50 Ways to Love Your Grandparents

Approaching the Heart with a Rational Mind

Sarah Cline, Ph.D.

Copyright © 2023 Sarah Cline, Ph.D.

All rights reserved.

The contents of this book may not be reproduced, duplicated, or transmitted without direct written permission from the author.

Under no circumstances will any legal responsibility or blame be held against the publisher for any reparation, damages, or monetary loss due to the information herein, either directly or indirectly.

Legal Notice:

This book is copyright-protected. This is only for personal use. You cannot amend, distribute, sell, use, quote, or paraphrase any part of the content within this book without the consent of the author.

Disclaimer Notice:

Please note the information contained within this document is for educational and entertainment purposes only. Every attempt has been made to provide accurate, up-to-date, and reliable complete information. No warranties of any kind are expressed or implied. Readers acknowledge that the author is not engaging in the rendering of legal, financial, medical, or professional advice. The content of this book has been derived from various sources. Please consult a licensed professional before attempting any techniques outlined in this book.

By reading this document, the reader agrees that under no circumstances is the author responsible for any losses, direct or indirect, which are incurred as a result of the use of the information contained within this document, including, but not limited to, errors, omissions, or inaccuracies.

ISBN: 978-1-937209-14-8

Contents

Introduction 1

1. Understanding Personality Types: A Deep Dive 4
   Origins of Personality Types
   Cave Dweller (CD) and Mountain Yeller (MY) Grandparents
   Deeper Dive into the Cave Dweller (CD) Grandparent
   Deeper Dive into the Mountain Yeller (MY) Grandparent
   The Straddler Grandparent
   Key Takeaways

2. Communication Is Key 21
   Express Feelings in a Way They Understand
   Put Down Your Phone—Participate in Active Listening
   Pick Up Your Phone—or Better Yet, Talk to Them in Person
   Use Neutral Language to Curb Arguments
   Understand That the Dynamic Continues to Shift for Them
   Understand and Respect Boundaries as New Transitions Occur
   Deal with Unresolved Childhood Issues Respectfully

      Check in with Them Often
      Share Personal Growth Moments Regularly
      Respect Their Space and Yours
      Key Takeaways

3. Emotional Closeness   46
      Talk to Them
      Don't Wait for Them to Take the Lead
      Offer Surprise Gestures
      Organize Family Get-Togethers as They Get Older
      Walk Down Memory Lane with Them
      Mail Them Letters
      Make New Memories
      Help Them with Technology
      Bring Them Thoughtful Gifts
      Offer to Help Them with Household Duties
      Key Takeaways

4. Celebrate Good Times   61
      Go to Their Home and Cook for Them
      Host Social Events or Gatherings
      Celebrate Important Holidays or Anniversaries Together
      Create Hand-Made Gifts
      Celebrate Them "Just Because"
      Thank Them for All That They've Done for You and Your Parents
      Remember Them on Father's Day and Mother's Day
      Recognize Their Achievements and Yours—Together
      Tell Your Grandparents You Love Them
      Share Life-Altering Moments with Them (Even the Bad Ones)

Key Takeaways

5. Appreciate Them — 77
   Celebrate Their Emotional Strengths
   Understand That They're Human—Just Like You
   Ask Them About Their Past
   Ask Them for Advice on Your Future Endeavors
   Become Their Friend
   Key Takeaways

6. Boundaries — 91
   Set Boundaries for Your Grandparents
   Ask for Advice and Listen When They Give It
   Give Them the Benefit of the Doubt During Misunderstandings and Understand They're from a Different Time
   Avoid Being Offensive with Your Language
   Don't Forget "You" Time
   Key Takeaways

7. Socializing with Your Grandparents as an Adult — 106
   Call Them Often
   Ask Them How They Are at Least Once a Week
   Hug Them
   Get Together for the Holidays
   Let Them Spend Time with Your Kids and Partner
   Treat Them to Dinner or Ice Cream
   Experience New Activities or Hobbies Together
   Take Them on a Multi-Generation Family Vacation
   Plan Family Game Nights
   Revisit Places of Significance
   Key Takeaways

8. Final Thoughts   124
    - Understanding the Depth of Personality
    - The Unwavering Commitment of Love
    - The Adaptive Nature of Lasting Love
    - Celebrating Diversity Through Unity
    - The Journey of Personal and Mutual Growth
    - The Boundless Horizons of Love
    - The Continuing Evolution of Your Love Story

Appendices   128
- Self-Assessment Questionnaire: Determine Whether You're a CD, MY, or Straddler.
- Personality Indicator Scores
- Using the Scoring Chart
- Cave Dweller Tendencies

Introduction

Welcome to *50 Ways to Love Your Grandparents*. If you've picked up this book, you may be navigating familial challenges, eager to enhance existing familial bonds, or just gearing up for what the future holds in your family life. Whatever the case, you've taken a significant step toward deeper understanding and connection—so, congratulations are in order.

Throughout this volume and larger series, we'll focus on three universal personality categories: the reserved Cave Dweller (CD), the outgoing Mountain Yeller (MY), and the Straddler, who exhibits mixed traits. Recognizing and understanding these types is crucial, as they shape family dynamics in untold ways. Our aim is to provide practical insights into fundamental personalities, ensuring you're better equipped to navigate and strengthen your familial relationships. What's more, you'll walk away with a better grasp of who you truly are—and by knowing yourself, you can offer more to your family.

Armed with the insights from this book, you'll not only interpret actions but also understand the deeper motivations behind them with greater ease. Prepare to see your grandparents—and perhaps yourself—in a whole new light...

The Power of Personalities

Ahead, we'll demystify the core attributes of CDs, MYs, and Straddlers, equipping you with insights to comprehend and appreciate the nuances of each type. Appreciating these differences allows you to interpret your grandparents' behaviors accurately within their unique personality context, thus avoiding flawed assumptions.

Too often in familial relationships, we mistakenly attribute conflicts and misunderstandings to a lack of love, empathy, or respect. Yet, more frequently, it's a simple gap in understanding. When we don't perceive the underlying personality traits driving our grandparents' actions, we can misinterpret their intentions, leading to undue tension. It's not always about agreeing or having the same viewpoint; it's about acknowledging and respecting these inherent differences. By recognizing the core personality traits of CDs, MYs, and Straddlers, we can better empathize with our grandparents, allowing our bond to fully flourish.

Before We Begin

50 Ways to Love Your Grandparents offers no quick fix or casual checklist. Instead, it emphasizes "love" as an active endeavor, demanding both attention and effort. While you'll find a great deal of guidance here, it's up to you to apply these insights authentically.

Engaging with this material will require introspection, and there will be moments that challenge your current understanding of your grandparents' perspectives—and everything else, for that matter. Yet, it's in these times of reflection and adjustment that true growth happens…and, here, the fruits of your labor could scarcely be sweeter—some real incentive.

Through patience and ongoing application, you're not just enhancing your bond but, rather, refining how you connect. How you live. How you nurture their souls. So, cherish the process, love yourself, and love your grandparents on a whole new level.

Before we begin, remind yourself: you're a masterpiece—and a work in progress.

Chapter One

Understanding Personality Types: A Deep Dive

Do you find yourself struggling to understand your grandparents' personality traits? Are you frustrated that they're so dissimilar to yours? Chances are, as a child, as your grandparents shared their wisdom, you embraced and enjoyed the differences they exhibited. But as your relationship developed, those differences may have become sources of confusion or concern for you as an adult grandchild.

Understanding personality types is an essential piece of the puzzle when seeking to understand your grandparents. Appreciating your elders means discovering their many layers and complexities, and all of them should garner your attention if you are to foster a nurturing and understanding environment.

In this chapter, we will discuss the personality types of the Cave Dweller grandparent, which we will refer to as CD, the Mountain Yeller or MY grandparent, and the Straddler grandparent. Learning about these three basic personality types will give you a clearer picture of the unique benefits and challenges each creates. And understanding is an essential first step to bringing harmony and happiness into your everyday life.

Origins of Personality Types

Long before the modern-day classifications of CDs and MYs and even before psychiatrists and psychologists stepped onto the scene, ancient civilizations sought to explain human behavior and its various nuances.

The Ancient Greeks

The ancient Greeks developed the theory of the "four humors" to explain the causes of health and illness, both mental and physical. This theory suggested that an individual's temperament was influenced by bodily fluids: blood (sanguine), yellow bile (choleric), black bile (melancholic), and phlegm (phlegmatic). The Greeks thought these humors were directly related to being sanguine (cheerful), choleric (short-tempered), melancholic (reserved), or phlegmatic (relaxed). Therefore, the balance of these humors was believed to influence an individual's temperament, health, and overall disposition. An imbalance of these humors led to behaviors that, today, we associate with certain mental illnesses. For example:

- Sanguine (blood) was associated with cheerful, optimistic, enthusiastic personality traits. An imbalance was thought to be due to a person having too much blood in their body, which would cause a person to be overly confident and exhibit impulsive behavior. Possible narcissistic and/or bipolar disorder.

- Choleric (yellow bile) was associated with being ambitious, passionate, and easily angered. An imbalance causes anger, irritability, or extremely aggressive behavior and rage. Possible borderline personality disorder.

- Melancholic (black bile) was associated with being thoughtful, reflective, and often sad or depressed. This imbalance was associated with melancholy and depression.

- Phlegmatic (phlegm) was associated with being calm, reliable, and often unemotional or apathetic. An imbalance was associated with lethargy, sluggishness, or a lack of motivation, which, much like melancholia, is a symptom of depression.

Treating these emotional ailments is where things got even more interesting. If the Greeks thought you had an imbalance of any of these four humors, you would likely have received one of the following treatments:

Dietary Changes: Prescribed depending on the humor in excess. For instance, someone deemed overly choleric might be advised to avoid hot or spicy foods that would "agitate" the yellow bile.

Bloodletting: If you were someone believed to have an excess of sanguine humor, it was common practice to be prescribed bloodletting. This process involved removing blood from the body by way of leeches or actual cutting.

Purging: In order to remove excess bile or phlegm, laxatives were used, as were emetics, which induced vomiting.

Baths/Sweating: To promote toxin removal, balms and ointments were applied to the skin to help with the imbalance of any of these four humors.

The Greeks' attempts to "treat" imbalances in personality or health were based on the observations and the knowledge they had at the time. The four humors theory was eventually replaced with more accurate medical models, but its influence can still be seen in some of our languages today.

The Introvert and The Extrovert

Carl Gustav Jung (1875–1961) was a Swiss psychiatrist, psychoanalyst, and the father of analytical psychology. He developed several concepts that had a profound influence on both psychology and popular culture. One of his most notable contributions was the concept of "introversion" and "extraversion" (often used in the more modern manner: introvert and extrovert). Jung's theory asserts that introversion and extraversion are attitudes that represent the direction in which a person's psychic energy flows.

Extraversion (Extrovert)

According to Jung, the extrovert's energy flows outward. This personality type is more oriented toward the external world and derives energy from interacting with its surroundings, including people, events, and situations. If you have an extroverted grandparent, they might tend to be more outgoing, social, and interested in external events. Extroverts are typically action-oriented and are generally more comfortable in social situations than introverts. Many extroverts are highly influenced by external factors and are occasionally prone to negative introspection.

Introversion (Introvert)

As the name suggests, the introvert's energy flows inward. Those with this personality type are more oriented toward their inner world, relying on introspection and internal reflection. If your grandparent is introverted, they are generally more reserved and often feel more comfortable with individual activities or smaller group settings. They derive energy and pleasure from thinking, daydreaming, or exploring ideas. Although an introverted senior's daily practices tend to lead to social isolation, many have a small number of deep connections with people of their choosing.

Jung believed that everyone has an introverted and extroverted side, with one being more dominant than the other. It's a spectrum, and while some might be near the extremes of that spectrum, most individuals lie somewhere in between.

Cave Dweller (CD) and Mountain Yeller (MY) Grandparents

While not strictly rooted in these historical contexts, the CD and MY classifications are evolved constructs reflecting the same human desire to understand ourselves and others in our world more deeply.

While our contemporary understanding of the CD and MY classifications doesn't stem directly from ancient Greek or Jungian theories, much like their historical counterparts, they are observed patterns in modern relationships. By identifying recurring patterns, we can forge tools to help us navigate and harmonize interpersonal interactions.

Deeper Dive into the Cave Dweller (CD) Grandparent

To determine whether you and your grandparents fall into the CD or MY category, we must first learn about their traits.

Reserved Nature

If your grandparent is a CD, they will predominantly showcase a calm and reserved demeanor. They are introspective and tend to hold their emotions close to their chest because they value their inner world and the sanctuary it provides. Their reserved nature doesn't mean that they are indifferent or detached; it just means that they process their emotions internally and over time.

For instance, after an argument, a CD grandparent might choose to withdraw to process their feelings rather than immediately confront an issue. They do this because they typically feel uncomfortable with strife and need time to work through their emotions and understand how to communicate their feelings.

Socially, a CD grandparent is often found in quieter corners, engaging in deep conversation with one or two individuals rather than in the center of a party. In group discussions, a CD will offer insights only if specifically asked or if they feel strongly about a topic.

Logical Thinking and Literal Communication

A CD grandparent leans more toward analytical and logical thinking. They make decisions only after careful contemplation and weighing the pros and cons. They work hard to keep their emotions from clouding their judgment. This logical thinking manifests in their communication, as they will get right to the point without inserting emotions or using stories to embellish their point.

For example, if you discuss a film with a CD grandparent, they will likely dissect plot points with impeccable logic and even point out strengths and weaknesses. But they might miss the emotional undertones of the movie. If you ask a CD if they liked the cake you brought for dessert, they might reply, "Yes," without diving into flowery descriptives.

It's important to note that a CD grandparent may also get frustrated with an embellished story that doesn't immediately get to the point. It doesn't mean they don't want to hear the story or don't care what the person has to say, their brain is just geared toward immediate outcomes.

Need for Space

A CD grandparent has an inherent need for both emotional and physical personal space. For them, requiring space is not about distancing themselves from loved ones, it's about needing solitude to recharge and reflect.

CD grandparents enjoy reading books in a cozy nook or going for solitary walks. They may listen to music while doing chores instead of talking. This alone time is essential for a CD grandparent, especially after a day filled with social interactions.

Singular Focus

A CD grandparent has unparalleled concentration when engrossed in a task and prefers completing that task to their satisfaction before tackling another.

If you attempt to talk to a CD grandparent while they're studying or sketching, for example, they may be so absorbed in what they're doing that you'll be tuned out. It's not that what you're saying is unimportant to them, it's just challenging for them to spread their focus on more than one thing at a time because they give each item their full attention.

Social Preferences

Traditionally, if your grandparent was labeled an introvert, many would also consider them anti-social. But that couldn't be farther from the truth. An introvert, or a CD grandparent, just leans toward more intimate social interactions. Large gatherings can leave a CD grandparent feeling overwhelmed and quickly drain their mental and emotional battery.

Emotional Processing

While CD grandparents might not outwardly express their emotions, they experience them deeply. However, their internal reflections may lead to a delay in their outward emotional expression. While a CD grandparent may seem distant after an emotional confrontation, many need to process the interaction before they react. A CD grandparent needs time to contemplate a disagreement, analyze the conversation, and figure out where things went wrong before they can move on to a resolution. This meditation is essential for a CD grandparent's family members to understand; the more they push them to express themselves, the more they will clam up in response.

Fears Regarding Loss of Security

Finally, if your grandparent is a CD, they will crave stability in their life. Driven by a sense of perfectionism, they might demonstrate caution in their decisions, often opting for paths with predictable outcomes and minimal risk. At times, this drive for perfection and achievement might see them prioritizing tasks such as studies over spending quality time with family. This isn't due to diminished affection but stems from an intrinsic need for accomplishment and security. The hierarchy of basic needs for a CD grandparent is as follows:

- Career/Financial Security (for those still active in such roles, or legacy and end-of-life planning for those who are not)
- Hobbies/Interests
- Relationships/Family
- Health/Wellness

This doesn't mean CD grandparents value their career more than their family. It just means that it's essential for a CD grandparent to feel that they're cementing a foundation of achievement and security before they can give their full attention to the next set of needs.

Deeper Dive into the Mountain Yeller (MY) Grandparent

If your grandparent is an extrovert, chances are they've been called that more than once in their lifetime. An extrovert is typically known for being outgoing and the life of any party. But there's so much more to them than meets the eye.

Outgoing Nature/Group Socialization

An MY grandparent is inherently outgoing. Their energy thrives on interactions and being around people as often as possible. Instead of needing time alone to recharge, an MY grandparent wants to be out and involved.

At a social event, MY grandparents will be the first to initiate games and dancing and will often bounce from person to person, catching up rather than focusing on one task at a time. Deep conversations are still on the table, but not at a social event. MY grandparents are usually the ones who rally their friends for a group outing over a weekend rather than sitting at home reading a book or watching TV. Even in the workplace, MY grandparents love group projects and find collaborative brainstorming and teamwork exciting.

Emotion-Driven

MY grandparents are heart ruled because they lead with their intuition and emotions. Being ruled by their heart doesn't mean their decisions are devoid of logic, but their feelings heavily influence their reactions. MY grandparents can be emotional during arguments but are also the first to send a heartfelt message to a friend upon hearing they are having a rough time.

An MY grandparent's emotions will show throughout their storytelling, so be patient when they tell you about an event or relay the plot to a movie. Chances are both will be full of details and embellishments.

Connection and Touch

MY grandparents value genuine connections and physical expressions of affection. Whether it's a warm hug, a gentle touch on the arm, or sitting closely on the couch, these gestures reinforce their feeling of being connected to their loved ones. In their relationships with family members, MY grandparents often cherish physical presence and acts of companionship as a top priority, viewing them as essential expressions of love and care. This aspect of their need for connection will be explored in depth a bit later.

Dynamic Focus

The MY grandparent is a natural multitasker. Instead of focusing on one task at a time, their attention shifts between assignments. They enjoy the energy they get from juggling multiple things and often get bored working on one project for an extended period. It can be common to find the MY grandparent drifting off during a long presentation. They're busy thinking about weekend plans.

The MY grandparent doesn't mind dealing with paperwork, but they'll work through it while watching television or listening to music. As for conversations, the MY grandparent loves to chat, but don't be surprised if you find the MY grandparent scrolling on their phone while talking with you. It's not that the MY grandparent thinks what you have to say is unimportant. Their mind simply runs at higher speeds, and they're more comfortable when processing more than one thing at a time.

Inferential Communication

The MY grandparent often communicates using stories, anecdotes, and metaphors rather than getting straight to the point. They rely on indirect implications and expect others to infer meanings, which can confuse some who may not be familiar with their communication style.

During an argument, the family of an MY grandparent may find it hard to decipher what the MY grandparent really wants, even if the grandparent feels they have told them directly. It's essential to have a middle ground where communication is concerned, especially if your grandparent is an MY trying to get through to a CD; their communication styles are very different.

Immediate Emotional Expression

Unlike their CD counterparts, MY grandparents are quick to express their emotions. They're an open book and rarely hesitate to share their feelings of joy and disappointment. This can be overwhelming for a CD who is uncomfortable with an emotional display.

One of the greatest fears the MY grandparent faces is the fear of rejection. If an MY grandparent has a CD grandchild, who usually pulls away at any sign of conflict, this can be a bone of contention. The MY grandparent will take your withdrawal as a sign of personal rejection. It's important to communicate that you are not rejecting them and that you simply need time to wrap your head around and process the disagreement. Give the MY grandparent verbal and physical affirmations whenever possible. The hierarchy of basic needs for the MY grandparent is as follows:

- Relationships/Family
- Hobbies/Interests
- Health/Wellness
- Career/Financial Security

If you are a CD and your grandparent is an MY, don't panic; it doesn't mean you cannot have a strong bond. There are plenty of amazing and fulfilling relationships between opposites. It just means it will take time, work, and patience to learn one another's needs and effectively communicate.

The Straddler Grandparent

If your grandparent is a Straddler, they are adaptable and enjoy the best of both worlds. They can immerse themselves in a book like a CD or be the life of a party like an MY. They possess an emotional agility that allows them to straddle their personality types seamlessly. While this book predominantly focuses on CD and MY grandparents, Straddlers can use it to understand the extremes and navigate their middle ground more effectively.

Excellent Balance Between Reflection and Expression

A Straddler grandparent can introspect like a CD, valuing quiet moments of thought. Yet, they also appreciate the expressive vitality of the MY and share their feelings and ideas openly when a situation calls for it. They are as happy spending a quiet evening reading as they are going to a book club and actively participating in a lively discussion.

Adaptable in Social Situations

While they might not always be the life of the party, they easily adjust to situations based on the social settings and the company involved. They can engage in a one-on-one conversation at a party and then join a group game or be the center of the party later in the evening.

Values Both Logic and Emotion

A Straddler grandparent approaches situations with a logical mindset but is equally attuned to the emotional undercurrents, valuing the importance of feelings in decision-making. For example, if a peer faces a personal issue, the Straddler grandparent will offer practical solutions while simultaneously providing emotional support.

Flexibility in Needs and Fears

The Straddler grandparent's hierarchy of needs will fluctuate based on circumstances, and they might experience fears from the CD's spectrum, such as loss of security, as well as the MY's fear of rejection. However, adaptability allows them to prioritize different aspects of their life. While working on an important business project, they will prioritize career stability, but in their downtime, they will focus on relationships and personal connections.

Fluid Communication Styles

A Straddler grandparent can communicate both directly and inferentially, often adjusting their communication based on the recipient. For example, when conversing with their analytical adult child, they will be direct and to the point, but when they talk to a grandchild, they become expressive and delve into all the nitty-gritty details.

Straddlers possess an innate ability to mediate and find common ground, especially in family dynamics where CDs and MYs might find themselves at odds. Their adaptability enables them to comprehend and empathize with both personality types, easing communication and diminishing misunderstandings.

A Straddler grandparent may seem like they have an effortless connection with their family members. However, everyone encounters their share of struggles. The flexibility of a Straddler often causes confusion about their preferences and needs. They might sometimes feel stretched or trapped in the middle, particularly in a polarized situation where they wish to please their family and struggle to voice their disagreements. A Straddler grandparent must discern what is truly significant to them while also learning to navigate their family members' personality types, much like everyone else.

So, How Do You Find Common Ground?

I'm a CD, and my grandparent is an MY; will we always be at odds?

Absolutely not! In this book, we don't tell you how to "cope" with your grandparent's differences. Instead, we empower you to recognize the unique strengths each personality type possesses. A CD's introspection can balance an MY's spontaneity. An MY's vivacity and exuberance can harmonize beautifully with a CD's depth and stability.

Recognizing these different traits is merely the first step to fostering a strong bond. The real challenge, and indeed the focus of this book, is to find ways to navigate the complexities of these interactions.

After all, the beauty of the grandparent-grandchild relationship truly unfolds in the dance between these personalities.

Key Takeaways

Diving into the intricacies of personality types isn't about affixing labels, but rather enriching our understanding. With these insights, you're now armed with the necessary vocabulary to navigate the labyrinth of human emotions and connections, fostering an environment where respect grows, comprehension deepens, and bonds strengthen. As we traverse this journey, let's remember that the goal isn't to change, but to adapt, understand, and love more deeply.

The foundation for a nurturing bond starts with understanding—understanding yourself, your grandparents, and the dynamics of your interactions. With the knowledge of CD and MY personality traits, you're well on your way to deepening that understanding, setting the stage for the subsequent chapters that will guide you on how to cherish your grandparents in ways that resonate with both of you.

Understanding personality differences is essential for nurturing compatibility. This chapter has illuminated the fundamental traits of CDs, MYs, and Straddlers.

- **Express, Don't Explode:** When speaking to your grandparents, articulate feelings carefully. Address issues directly, focusing on one topic at a time.

- **Listen and Hear:** Actively listening to your grandparents means more than just catching their words. Engage deeply, decipher underlying feelings, and resonate with their emotions.

- **Narrate Neutrally:** Use "I" and "we" statements when discussing family matters. These phrases are more than just words; they pave the way for understanding without triggering defenses.

- **Pivot Your Approach:** Understand the value CDs place on silence for introspection, and amplify the natural vibrancy of MYs with affirming words.

- **Establish Clear Boundaries:** Set them. Honor them. If your grandparent has boundaries differing from yours, embrace them. Engage in dialogues to find common ground.

- **Initiate Family Check-Ins:** Regular reflections on your bond with your grandparents provide direction. Treat these moments as opportunities for growth, not confrontations. And when they seek alone time, respect it—solitude is essential for personal insight.

- **Share, Grow, Connect:** Narrate personal stories of growth and challenges with your grandparents. It's not just about sharing experiences—it's about intertwining your familial narratives.

The key is understanding and complementing each other's rhythms. When personalities harmonize through understanding and respect, relationships flourish.

Chapter Two

Communication Is Key

Communication serves as the bedrock of any enduring grandparent-grandchild bond. It is the crucial bridge that allows for a meaningful connection across various personality types. This chapter is dedicated to enhancing your communication skills and will help you to comprehend and acknowledge the unique needs and individuality of your grandparents.

While the assumption that relationships between grandparents and grandchildren are inherently strong can be reassuring, fostering a deep and lasting connection requires deliberate action, reciprocal respect, and a profound willingness to understand. This goes beyond a basic awareness of your grandparents' favorite activities or interests; it demands an in-depth engagement with their distinct personalities and how these traits interact with yours.

In a time when digital communication often replaces in-depth personal interactions, the significance of genuine human contact must not be overlooked. Patience, thoughtfulness, and attentive presence are indispensable elements of a robust relationship. As you delve into this chapter, take the time to pause, reflect, and truly internalize the information presented. Open and respectful dialogue does more than maintain a relationship, it builds a vibrant emotional link between you and your grandchildren. The following strategies will provide guidance on expressing your feelings effectively and fostering a nurturing bond.

Express Feelings in a Way They Understand

Understanding and conveying emotions in a way that resonates with your grandparents is crucial, whether they are introverted CDs, extroverted MYs, or adaptable Straddlers. It requires choosing words and expressions that align with their unique experiences and comprehension. Avoid confusing slang or colloquialisms, and opt for clear, concrete language instead.

When sharing feelings with CD grandparents, who are likely reserved by nature, use straightforward statements. For lively MY grandparents, add colorful details and examples that capture the emotion's intensity. With flexible Straddlers, gauge their mood and adapt your style accordingly.

Using "I" statements clarifies your feelings without making assumptions about your grandparents. For instance, "I feel overwhelmed when my workload is too heavy" is better than "You don't understand my busy life." This invites your grandparents to engage without defensiveness.

Be patient as CD grandparents introspectively process what you've shared. MY grandparents may respond more quickly and effusively. Straddlers' reactions will vary. Appreciate the subtleties in their communication style.

Make sure the conversation is reciprocal by taking time to understand their feelings too. Create an open environment where CDs, MYs, and Straddlers alike feel comfortable expressing themselves. Tailor your approach to resonate with their unique personality type, ensuring mutual understanding.

Communicate Clearly and Directly

When discussing sensitive issues with your grandparents, clarity is key. Avoid ambiguous language that can cause confusion. Speak plainly about issues to help them understand your perspective and needs.

Stay on Topic

Discussions can get heated, and it's sometimes tempting to bring up past issues. This is akin to what Dr. John M. Gottman describes as the "kitchen sink effect," where everything except the kitchen sink is thrown into the conversation, cluttering it with unrelated problems. To maintain a productive dialogue, focus on the current topic.

Overcome the "Kitchen Sink Effect"

In moments of tension, it's easy to fall into the pattern of rehashing the past, which Dr. Gottman's research shows can undermine effective communication. This often occurs for two main reasons:

- An instinctive but counterproductive desire to "win" the argument can lead to bringing up past grievances, which may provide a momentary sense of victory but can harm the long-term relationship with your grandparents.

- Inadequate communication skills often contribute to this problem. Without the tools to address unresolved feelings, it's easy to let them spill over into current conversations.

Remember, bringing up the past can divert the discussion and leave the actual issue at hand unresolved. If you find yourself tempted to recount previous arguments, consider whether you might be avoiding the actual issue.

Prioritize constructive dialogue over winning an argument. Aim for understanding and cooperation, staying engaged in the present conversation. To build a lasting and harmonious relationship, address issues with careful consideration.

Avoid Negative Tactics

Personal attacks and manipulative strategies should never be part of your conversations. Such tactics can only drive an emotional wedge between you and your grandparents. Strive for resolution, not victory, in your communications.

Put Down Your Phone—Participate in Active Listening

Older generations typically have a very different relationship with screens and technology than younger people. For many in the older demographic, face-to-face conversation and direct phone calls have been the primary modes of communication for most of their lives. They may view the omnipresence of screens and the constantly divided attention they bring as a barrier to genuine connection.

Putting down your phone is a symbolic and practical gesture that signals to your grandparents that they have your full attention. It removes the distractions that often lead to superficial engagement.

Younger people constantly checking their phones may be perceived as a sign of disinterest or disrespect. The act of putting down your phone in the presence of your grandparents is not just about removing a distraction, but also about demonstrating respect for their preferred style of communication. It signals a willingness to engage on their terms and acknowledges the value of their presence and conversation.

Active listening is a technique that requires the listener to fully concentrate, understand, respond, and then remember what is being said. It is an essential component of effective communication and involves several key behaviors. Active listening demands you engage with the speaker without the interference of technology or other distractions.

Maintain eye contact, nod to acknowledge you are following, and offer small verbal affirmations such as "I see" or "I understand." This nonverbal communication shows that you are engaged in the conversation. Pay attention not only to the words but also to the tone of voice and body language, which can convey nuances of meaning that words alone may not capture.

Active listening across generational and personality divides requires an understanding of the distinct communication styles and preferences of older adults. For introverted CDs, putting down one's phone and eliminating distractions is crucial. This simple act shows respect and allows for a listening environment where CDs can share their thoughts without competing against technological interruptions.

When it comes to extroverted MYs, active listening can include managing their inclination to dominate the dialogue. Techniques such as taking deliberate pauses and summarizing what has been said encourage MYs to engage in a more balanced conversation. A reflective response to an MY might be, "You seem excited about that event, what stood out to you the most?"

Straddlers require a hybrid approach, catering to their mix of introverted and extroverted tendencies. A Straddler might appreciate a reflective statement that acknowledges both the content and the emotional undertone of their message, such as, "It seems like you enjoyed the quiet moments as much as the social aspects at the event."

To enhance focus for all personality types, it is beneficial to minimize potential distractions ahead of time. This might involve choosing a conducive environment for conversation or silencing electronic devices to prevent interruptions.

When engaging in active listening with older adults, it's also important to listen without judgment and not offer unsolicited advice. Reflective listening involves paraphrasing the speaker's words to show understanding and empathy, which is essential when communicating across different age groups and personality types. For instance, if a grandparent expresses a viewpoint from a bygone era, a nonjudgmental, reflective response might be, "That perspective is interesting, it reflects a different time."

Active listening is a respectful acknowledgment of the speaker's worth and a foundational practice for effective intergenerational communication. It requires the listener to be fully present and engaged, fostering a stronger connection and understanding between the younger and older generations.

It is important to avoid interrupting while they are speaking. Wait for a natural pause to ask clarifying questions or offer your perspective. This patience allows for a deeper exchange of thoughts and feelings.

Active listening also means withholding judgment and refraining from offering unsolicited advice. Your grandparents might share opinions you disagree with or that are from a different time. In these instances, active listening involves giving space to those opinions, seeking to understand where they are coming from, and responding with empathy.

Pick Up Your Phone—or Better Yet, Talk to Them in Person

In an era where the ping of a notification often takes precedence over the ring of a telephone, the art of voice communication is at risk of being lost. Picking up the phone and calling someone has become an almost radical act of personal connection. It's important to recognize that, for older generations, this simple act can be a significant gesture of care and respect.

A phone call is immediate and engaging. Unlike a text message, it doesn't sit unread or answered at the recipient's convenience; it demands attention here and now. For the person on the other end, especially if they're from an older generation, it says, "You are important to me at this moment." This mode of communication also allows for a rich exchange of emotions through the subtleties of voice—something that emoticons and GIFs struggle to convey.

When we speak on the phone, our focus is sharpened. Without the visual cues available in face-to-face interactions, we listen more intently to the tone, pitch, and pace of the speaker's voice. This form of active engagement is essential for truly understanding the emotional undercurrents of a conversation. For those who grew up in a time when long-distance calls were a luxury and a letter took days to deliver, a phone call is not just a means of communication—it's a bridge across distances, a shared moment in time.

Yet, if a phone call is a bridge, then a face-to-face conversation is the destination it leads to. In-person dialogue is where the full spectrum of human communication comes to life. Facial expressions, gestures, and postures are all integral to the way we interpret messages. In the presence of another, we can catch the furrow of a brow or the crinkle of eyes in laughter—subtleties that tell us more than words alone.

For many in older generations, face-to-face interaction is the epitome of respect and engagement. It is a demonstration that we are willing to give something increasingly scarce—our undistracted time and physical presence. In-person, we can't hide behind screens or delay our responses. We are compelled to be present in the most literal sense, fostering a level of intimacy and trust that digital communication can't replicate.

In-person conversations allow for a shared environment. Whether it's a walk in the park or a quiet sit-down in a living room, the setting contributes to the conversation. Shared activities or environments can stir memories, prompt stories, and build a common ground that strengthens relationships.

Thus, in navigating our communication with different generations, it's essential to balance convenience and connection. While a text or email might suffice for quick updates or sharing links to articles of interest, they should not replace the personal touch of a phone call or the depth of an in-person chat. When we attempt to connect in these more traditional ways, we honor the preferences of those who appreciate them and foster stronger, more meaningful relationships.

Use Neutral Language to Curb Arguments

Effective communication across generational divides often hinges on the ability to maintain composure and express oneself without inciting conflict. Utilizing neutral language is a pivotal strategy for curbing arguments and facilitating understanding. Neutral language is devoid of charged emotions, accusations, and personal biases, making it an indispensable tool in intergenerational discussions where differing viewpoints are often at play.

Neutral language involves the deliberate choice of words that are unbiased and non-confrontational. It is about stating facts without the addition of subjective judgments. For instance, instead of saying, "You never understand what I'm saying," a neutral alternative would be, "It seems we have a misunderstanding; let's clarify our points." This approach doesn't place blame but opens up a space for dialogue.

Another aspect of using neutral language is to avoid absolutes such as "always" or "never," which may not be accurate and can escalate tensions. These words can make the receiver feel attacked and defensive, shutting down any potential for productive conversation. A statement such as "You always forget to call me back" could be reframed as "I've noticed there have been times when you haven't returned my calls."

Questions can also be framed neutrally to encourage openness and prevent defensiveness. Asking "What's your view on this?" instead of "Why can't you see it my way?" invites a sharing of perspectives without implying that there is a right or wrong stance.

Active listening plays a significant role in employing neutral language. By attentively listening to the other person, we can reflect their thoughts and feelings in our responses, ensuring that our words are considerate and pertinent to the conversation. For example, "I understand you're concerned about this issue, let's examine the possible outcomes together."

The tone of voice is equally important. A calm tone conveys respect and willingness to engage, whereas a raised or tense voice may convey aggression or impatience. Nonverbal cues, such as maintaining eye contact and open body language, complement the use of neutral language by showing a genuine interest in the conversation.

Neutral language facilitates a respectful exchange of ideas and perspectives. It allows individuals from different generations to navigate sensitive topics without triggering emotional responses that could lead to disputes. By focusing on clarity, respect, and a shared goal of understanding, neutral language becomes a powerful tool in bridging the communication gap between generations, fostering harmony and mutual respect.

The words you choose are important. They can either invite open communication or lead to defensiveness. To facilitate a constructive conversation, it's beneficial to concentrate on the specific behavior or event and communicate the impact it has on you. This can be effectively done through "We" statements and "I" statements.

Employ "We" Statements for Teamwork

Introducing "we" statements frames the situation as a shared concern, promoting a sense of partnership. It suggests that you are both on the same side and working toward a common goal, which can diffuse tension and foster a willingness to find a middle ground.

Avoid saying:
"You never seem to understand how to use the new technology I set up for you; it feels like you don't even try."

Try this approach:
"We both know technology can be tricky, and I see you're having some trouble with the new setup. How about we go over it together so it's easier for you?"

This reframing presents the issue as a mutual aim, avoiding blame and encouraging a cooperative solution.

Implement "I" Statements to Express Personal Feelings

"I" statements allow you to convey how you are affected by certain actions without casting blame. This approach, supported by mental health professionals, provides a way for you to express your feelings and needs respectfully and openly.

Avoid saying:
"You keep questioning my career choices, which is really annoying."

Try this instead:
"I feel stressed when my career choices are questioned. I value your opinion, but I also need to make my own decisions. Can we discuss this with respect for each other's viewpoints?"

By focusing on your own experiences and emotions, you reduce the chance of your grandchildren becoming defensive, paving the way for a more empathetic and productive exchange. Using both "We" and "I" statements can lead to a dialogue that is more honest, less confrontational, and encourages mutual understanding and empathy without casting aspersions or assigning fault.

Understand That the Dynamic Continues to Shift for Them

Adapting to the developing dynamics of relationships across generations is crucial, as change is a constant in human interactions. Recognizing that the context in which older generations perceive and interact with the world is in constant flux is key to understanding and empathizing with their experiences. This understanding is vital in maintaining healthy and supportive relationships.

As individuals age, their roles and expectations within a family or community often shift. Retirement, health issues, and changes in social status can significantly alter their day-to-day experiences and needs. It's important to acknowledge that what was once a given in their lives may no longer be the case. The grandparent who was once a provider may now need support; the confident decision-maker may now face insecurities about the future.

These transitions can be challenging, and it's important for younger family members or friends to remain cognizant of these shifts. By doing so, they can provide the appropriate level of empathy and support. It involves staying informed about their changing interests, abilities, and the way they choose to engage with others and the world around them.

For example, a person who used to be the life of the party might now prefer quieter gatherings. Recognizing this change and planning family events that accommodate their current comfort levels shows understanding and respect for their evolving preferences.

Similarly, changes in technology and communication can be disorienting for older generations. What seems like a simple update to a smartphone user interface can be a significant hurdle for someone who didn't grow up with such technology. Offering patience and help, rather than frustration or dismissal, can help them navigate these changes more confidently.

The dynamic also shifts in terms of dependency and care. An adult child may find themselves in a caregiver role, which can be a significant transition for both parties. It's essential to have open conversations about these changes, discussing the implications and emotions that come with them and finding a path forward that maintains everyone's dignity and autonomy.

Understanding that the dynamic continues to shift allows for a compassionate approach to the evolving nature of intergenerational relationships. It requires ongoing dialogue, a readiness to adjust one's own expectations, and a commitment to recognizing and adapting to the new realities faced by older generations. With this approach, it is possible to foster a relationship that is flexible, supportive, and respectful of the continual changes in life's journey.

Understand and Respect Boundaries as New Transitions Occur

Establishing and respecting boundaries is a fundamental aspect of any healthy relationship, and this becomes even more critical as new transitions occur within the lives of older generations. As they navigate through changes such as retirement, shifts in health, or alterations in their living situations, it's important to recognize and honor their need for boundaries.

As transitions unfold, individuals may reassess what they are comfortable with in terms of personal space, time commitments, and emotional capacity. For younger family members or friends, it's essential to seek clarity on these evolving boundaries rather than making assumptions based on past dynamics. Openly discussing these limits respects the autonomy of the individual and ensures that support is provided in a manner that is welcomed.

For example, someone who has recently retired may explore new hobbies or social groups. While they may appreciate invitations to family events, they may also value time to pursue these new interests. Respecting their decision to decline an invitation without pressure or guilt allows them to establish a healthy balance between family time and personal growth.

Similarly, as health changes, so might preferences around physical contact and activities. A grandparent who once enjoyed spirited play with grandchildren may now require quieter interactions. Respecting this new boundary means creating environments and activities that are inclusive of their current capabilities, ensuring they can still take part fully and joyfully in family life.

Besides respecting physical and time boundaries, it's also important to understand emotional boundaries. The need for privacy, particularly during vulnerable times, should be honored. If an older individual is dealing with health issues, they may not wish to discuss the details extensively. Giving them the space to share at their own pace, on their own terms, is a form of profound respect.

The establishment of new boundaries is not a one-time event; it is an ongoing process that requires continuous attention and sensitivity. It involves actively listening, being observant, and sometimes simply asking how best to provide support during a period of change.

Respecting these boundaries does not just preserve the individual's sense of self but also strengthens the trust and understanding within the relationship.

By understanding and respecting boundaries as new transitions occur, you can provide the kind of support that truly honors the person's evolving journey. It's about creating a safe space for them to navigate their changing world, knowing that their loved ones are allies in their autonomy and advocates for their well-being.

Deal with Unresolved Childhood Issues Respectfully

Addressing unresolved childhood issues within the context of intergenerational relationships is a delicate task that requires tact, empathy, and a respectful approach. For many older adults, childhood experiences have had a lasting impact on their perceptions and behaviors, and these issues may resurface as they age. When these matters come to light, it's crucial for family members and caregivers to engage with understanding and not judgment.

Understanding the Roots

Before initiating a conversation, take time to understand your feelings. Reflect on the specific events from your childhood that have left a lasting impact. Are there particular patterns of behavior or incidents that have sown seeds of resentment or misunderstanding? Acknowledging these elements to yourself first is crucial.

Creating a Safe Space for Dialogue

Recognizing whether a grandparent is a CD, MY, or Straddler can guide the creation of an environment conducive to open communication. CD individuals may prefer quiet settings, perhaps a comfortable living room with minimal distractions, to feel at ease during sensitive discussions. MYs might respond better in a more dynamic setting, perhaps during a walk in the park or while engaging in a shared activity, such as gardening, which can provide a natural flow to the conversation.

The first step in dealing with unresolved childhood issues is to acknowledge their presence and validity. Addressing unresolved issues from your own childhood with your grandparents requires sensitivity and a thoughtful approach tailored to different personality types. To create a conducive environment for such discussions, consider settings and activities that align with your mutual preferences. If you're both introverted, a quiet space might be ideal, such as a cozy corner at home with a photo album to jog memories. For more extroverted pairs, a walk in a familiar park or a shared hobby session can provide a natural backdrop for conversation.

Navigating the delicate waters of unresolved childhood issues with your grandparents requires a blend of sensitivity, patience, and clear communication. These issues, if left unaddressed, can silently affect your relationship. As an adult grandchild, the way you broach these matters can pave the path to understanding or widen the gap of disconnect. Here's how you can approach this sensitive topic:

Starting the Conversation

Begin with expressing your current feelings without pointing fingers at the past. You might start with, "I've been thinking about how we interact, and I feel like there are things I've carried with me I'd like to understand better and talk to you about."

Using Empathetic Language

Use "I" statements to express your feelings without laying blame. For instance:

- "I feel a bit hurt when I think about times I didn't feel heard as a child. Can you share your thoughts on this?"
- "I sometimes feel that there were expectations I couldn't meet. It would mean a lot to me to hear your perspective."

Listening Actively

After you've shared, give your grandparent the floor. Listen actively and without interruption. This shows respect for their perspective and encourages a more open dialogue.

Seeking Understanding, Not Solutions

Remember, the goal is not to find immediate solutions, but to understand each other better. You might say, "I'm not looking for apologies or explanations; I just want us to understand each other more."

When to Seek Professional Help

If the conversation takes a hard turn or you feel emotions are too high to handle alone, it may be time to suggest professional help. Approach this gently, emphasizing that it's not about placing blame but about seeking understanding and healing together. Suggesting a therapist who specializes in family dynamics can be helpful.

Propose it positively, for example, "I think it could really help us both to have a guide through this conversation. What do you think about us talking to someone together?"

Continuing the Conversation

Issues aren't usually resolved in one sitting. Agree to keep the lines of communication open, and schedule regular check-ins to revisit the conversation if needed.

Respecting Their Response

Regardless of the outcome, respect your grandparent's response. They may need time to process or may not be ready to address certain issues. Respect their pace and space.

Encouraging Moments of Shared Growth

When progress is made, acknowledge it. Share moments of personal growth and invite them to do the same. This can help strengthen your bond and foster mutual respect and understanding.

In dealing with unresolved childhood issues respectfully, you are not just seeking to heal the child within, but also to deepen the adult relationship you share with your grandparents. It's about moving forward with empathy and a willingness to understand the complexities of each other's experiences. Remember, seeking professional help is a sign of strength and commitment to the health of your relationship.

Check in with Them Often

Regular check-ins with older adults are not just a matter of courtesy but a critical component of maintaining a healthy and supportive relationship. These check-ins serve as a barometer for their well-being, a means to pre-emptively address concerns, and a way to reinforce the bond of trust and care.

To effectively check in with older adults, establish a routine that fits comfortably into their schedule. Consistency in communication shows reliability and forms a structure that they can look forward to and rely upon. Whether it's a daily text message, a weekly video call, or bi-weekly in-person visits, the key is regularity and predictability.

During these check-ins, it's important to engage in meaningful conversation. Ask open-ended questions that go beyond the surface level, such as "What's something you've enjoyed this week?" or "Have there been any new challenges lately?" Such questions encourage deeper conversation and convey genuine interest in their lives.

It's also crucial to pay attention to non-verbal cues during these interactions. Changes in demeanor, mood, or energy levels can be indicators of underlying issues. If you notice any concerning signs, gently inquire if there's anything they would like to talk about or if there's any way you can support them.

These check-ins are not just about monitoring your grandparents' well-being; they also provide an opportunity for older adults to feel heard and valued. Sharing your own experiences and updates can foster a mutual exchange, making it clear that this relationship is reciprocal and not merely out of obligation.

Be mindful that some older adults may have a tendency to downplay their struggles to avoid being a burden. Encourage honest dialogue by being empathetic and by sharing your own vulnerabilities. This can help create an environment where they feel safe to express their concerns without fear of judgment.

Lastly, while regular check-ins are important, they should not be intrusive. Respect your grandparents' independence and privacy, ensuring that your efforts to check in are balanced with their need for autonomy. By doing so, you respect their dignity while providing them with the assurance that they are not alone.

Share Personal Growth Moments Regularly

Fostering a relationship that thrives on mutual growth and understanding involves sharing personal achievements and moments of self-improvement. For older adults, hearing about the personal growth of loved ones can be a source of joy and can inspire them to engage in their own reflective practices.

When sharing your personal growth moments, it's essential to communicate in a way that resonates with their experiences and perspectives. For instance, discussing a newfound hobby might echo their memories of discovering passions during different life stages.

This not only bridges generational gaps but also encourages a two-way dialogue about life's evolving interests.

Describe your journey toward personal growth with clarity and sincerity. Whether it's overcoming a challenge at work, developing a new skill, or cultivating a healthier lifestyle, these narratives provide opportunities for older adults to connect with your life in meaningful ways. It helps them see your vulnerabilities and strengths, creating a deeper bond.

It's equally important to be an active listener when they share their experiences. Older adults often have rich stories of resilience and adaptation. By celebrating their past and present accomplishments, you reinforce their sense of self-worth and acknowledge the wisdom they have accumulated over the years.

In sharing these stories, be mindful of language and context. Avoid jargon or contemporary references that may not be familiar to them. Instead, focus on the emotions and lessons learned, which are universal and more easily understood.

Remember to share not just successes, but also the struggles that led to them. This honesty about the process of growth fosters a realistic and relatable narrative. It can encourage older adults to open up about their own challenges and aspirations, knowing that the path to personal growth is not always linear.

Regularly sharing such moments can also inspire older adults to pursue their own goals and hobbies, regardless of age. It's a reminder that growth and learning are lifelong processes. By including them in your journey, you offer motivation and, in return, gain an appreciative audience for your life's unfolding story.

Respect Their Space and Yours

Navigating the delicate balance of togetherness and independence is vital for maintaining healthy relationships with older adults. Respecting space—both theirs and yours—is a cornerstone of this equilibrium. It's about recognizing and honoring the need for personal time and the freedom to pursue individual interests.

For older adults, having their own space can be synonymous with retaining autonomy and dignity. It's important to support their desire for solitude or independent activities without imposing a sense of neglect. Communicate openly about their needs for privacy and ensure they feel comfortable asserting their boundaries.

Simultaneously, it's crucial to establish and articulate your own space requirements. Clear communication about your own boundaries not only serves your well-being but also models how to maintain healthy personal limits. This reciprocal understanding helps prevent feelings of suffocation or resentment that can arise from unspoken expectations.

When discussing plans or visits, be proactive in discussing how much time will be spent together. Offer options that allow them to choose based on their comfort and energy levels. It's also beneficial to have a mutual understanding that plans can be flexible, accommodating the ebb and flow of each person's need for space.

In shared living situations, create physical spaces that are designated as personal retreats. Even in communal settings, having a corner or a room where one can be alone is essential. Encourage the personalization of these spaces to reflect individual tastes and interests, which reinforces the concept of personal sanctuary.

Remember, respecting space extends beyond the physical. It includes giving them the mental and emotional room to process their thoughts and feelings independently. It means not pressing for conversations or interactions when they are not ready, and not taking it personally if they need a moment for themselves.

Ultimately, respecting space is an ongoing practice of mindfulness and consideration. It's about fostering an environment where everyone feels their need for independence is understood and valued. By doing so, you create a foundation of trust and respect that enhances the quality of your shared experiences.

Key Takeaways

Effective communication with older adults is a nuanced art that reflects respect, understanding, and adaptability. It's about creating a dialogue that resonates with their unique personality, whether they are introspective CDs, expressive MYs, or adaptable Straddlers.

- **Adapt to Their Language:** Convey emotions in ways that align with their personality type, ensuring clarity and comprehension for CDs, MYs, and Straddlers alike.

- **Embrace Active Listening:** Regardless of personality type, show genuine engagement by fully focusing on the conversation, validating their feelings, and responding thoughtfully.

- **Moderate the Screen Time:** Understand the generational differences in technology use and be present—both for tech-savvy MYs who might appreciate digital communication and for CDs who may prefer less screen interference.

- **Communicate In-Person:** Prioritize face-to-face interactions to foster stronger connections with CDs, who may value quiet presence, and with MYs and Straddlers who thrive on direct engagement.

- **Neutral Language:** Use "I" statements to facilitate open dialogue and reduce defensiveness. This is especially important when dealing with the sensitive CDs or the more outspoken Mys.

- **Recognize Shifting Dynamics:** Be aware that as people age, their personality traits may evolve, and be prepared to adjust your communication style with CDs, Mys, or Straddlers accordingly.

- **Respect Boundaries:** Honor the personal space and limits of CDs, who may cherish their solitude, and ensure Mys and Straddlers feel their need for interaction is equally respected.

- **Address Past Issues with Care:** Approach unresolved issues with a sensitivity that allows CDs to open up in their own time, while being direct yet considerate with Mys, and flexible with Straddlers.

- **Regular Check-ins:** Maintain frequent communication that acknowledges the preferred style of each personality type, whether it's quiet check-ins for CDs, more animated exchanges for MYs, or a balanced approach for Straddlers.

- **Share Growth:** Encourage open sharing of personal development, which resonates with the introspective nature of CDs, the expressive nature of MYs, and the balanced Straddlers.

- **Individual Space:** Respect the independence of CDs by supporting their need for alone time, give MYs room for their expansive energy, and allow Straddlers the flexibility they crave.

By embracing these practices, you foster a relationship built on mutual respect, deep understanding, and a communication style that adapts to the varied needs of CDs, MYs, and Straddlers. It's not about one-size-fits-all, it's about customizing your approach to resonate with the unique frequencies of their personalities.

Chapter Three

Emotional Closeness

As grandparents age, the dynamic of your relationship with them may shift. It is easy for physical distance and busy lives to create an emotional gap. However, maintaining a close bond is essential for their emotional well-being and can enrich your life as well. This chapter delves into practical ways to cultivate and sustain emotional closeness with your aging grandparents. From engaging in heartfelt conversations to helping with technology, we'll explore how simple acts can significantly deepen your connection. Whether it's through surprise gestures or walking down memory lane, these strategies foster intimacy and ensure your grandparents feel valued, loved, and supported.

Talk to Them

Starting a conversation with your grandparents is a gateway to intimacy that surpasses the mundane updates of daily life. It's about creating a space where experiences and emotions are exchanged, fostering a deeper understanding and bond.

For MY grandparents, conversations are an open stage. They thrive on the energy of animated storytelling and enthusiastic dialogue.

Engage them with topics that ignite their passion—be it a recent event or a fond memory. Ask open-ended questions that invite them to elaborate, showcase their experiences, and share their wisdom. They love to feel heard and to hold the spotlight in a grandchild's life.

CD grandparents might prefer a more subdued approach. They often express themselves in a more measured and reflective manner. To connect with them, choose a quiet setting and dive into topics that allow for contemplation and depth. For example, you could share a book you've read or discuss a movie that moved you. The key is to give them time to formulate their thoughts, to listen actively, and to show that you value their insights.

Straddlers, with their fluid nature, enjoy the best of both worlds. They can be as vivacious as MYs or as contemplative as CDs, depending on the environment and their mood. When engaging Straddlers, be versatile. Bring energy to the conversation when they seem up for a lively chat, or slow down when they're in a reflective state. Mirror their pace and be present, showing that you can ride the waves of their conversational needs with ease.

The act of talking to your grandparents is not merely about the exchange of words but about connecting with them on their terms, respecting their personality type, and enriching the tapestry of your relationship with every conversation.

Don't Wait for Them to Take the Lead

Fostering a sense of emotional closeness with your grandparents often requires you to be the one who starts contact and activities. This proactive stance can significantly strengthen the intergenerational bond, particularly when tailored to their personality types and acknowledging the nuances of generational differences.

For CD grandparents, who may naturally shy away from initiating contact because of their introverted tendencies, your willingness to reach out can bridge the gap that often forms from their hesitance. When engaging with them, it's helpful to incorporate activities that align with their interests, which may include quieter, more intimate settings. A key generational consideration is to ensure that invitations to connect are extended in a manner they're comfortable with—perhaps through a phone call rather than a text message, which may feel more personal and direct to older generations.

MY grandparents still relish the moments their grandchildren take the lead in communication. They might enjoy being introduced to new technology or social platforms that allow for a richer, more modern way of interaction, bridging the generational divide with shared experiences. However, it's important to walk them through these new methods patiently, respecting that they come from a time when face-to-face and telephonic communication were the norms.

Straddlers appreciate a balanced approach. They are the middle ground, often comfortable with both old and new ways of communication. Suggesting a mix of activities—some that harken back to their past, such as flipping through photo albums, and others that engage with the present, such as a video call—can cater to their flexible nature while respecting generational differences.

It's also important to be aware of the content of your conversations. Grandparents may have a wealth of experiences and wisdom to share, and showing interest in their stories and perspectives can make them feel valued. Conversely, sharing your own experiences and views can help them gain insight into your world, fostering a deeper understanding across the generational gap.

By taking the initiative and tailoring your approach to suit both their personality and generational background, you can create a more fulfilling and reciprocal relationship with your grandparents, one where they feel actively involved in your life and you in theirs.

Offer Surprise Gestures

Surprise gestures are a delightful way to express love and appreciation for your grandparents, creating spontaneous moments of joy that resonate deeply with their sense of being cherished. When considering such gestures, it's beneficial to tailor them to your grandparents' personality types and generational preferences.

For CD grandparents, who might appreciate subtlety and thoughtfulness, a surprise could be as simple as a handwritten note tucked into a book they're reading or a special edition of a newspaper they enjoy. The key is to deliver warmth without overwhelming them. CDs, typically being more reserved, may value gestures that acknowledge their need for a quieter form of engagement.

MY grandparents usually enjoy a more exuberant display of affection. Organizing a surprise visit from an old friend or arranging a small flash mob with family members to celebrate their favorite song can be thrilling experiences for them. Mys often love sharing stories and a big gesture gives them a new story to tell, connecting with their extroverted nature.

Straddlers will appreciate a balanced approach to surprises, perhaps a spontaneous day trip to a beloved place that combines the comfort of the familiar with the excitement of an unexpected outing. They enjoy the best of both worlds, and a gesture that recognizes their flexible nature can be particularly touching.

When considering generational preferences, remember that many grandparents cherish tradition. A surprise that brings back a sense of nostalgia, such as playing a song from their youth or recreating a meal from a significant time in their lives, can bridge the gap between past and present.

In any case, the element of surprise should always be handled with care, considering the health and temperament of your grandparents. A well-thought-out gesture, mindful of their personalities and the times they come from, not only brings immediate happiness but also strengthens the bonds of love and family.

Organize Family Get-Togethers as They Get Older

Organizing family get-togethers can become increasingly important as grandparents age. These events can serve as vital touchpoints for connection, reaffirming your grandparents' role and legacy within the family. When planning these gatherings, consider the personality types and generational perspectives of your grandparents to ensure the event is comfortable and enjoyable for them.

For CD grandparents, intimate and quiet settings may be more appealing. Small, cozy gatherings with close family members where everyone can engage in deep conversations might be most rewarding for them. CDs often prefer meaningful one-on-one interactions, so creating spaces at the event where these can happen naturally will help them feel connected without being overwhelmed.

MY grandparents might relish larger, more boisterous reunions. They often thrive amid laughter, storytelling, and group activities. For MYs, the joy of being surrounded by family and engaging in lively discussions or games can be invigorating. Consider having a dedicated space for them to entertain and be the center of attention if they wish.

Straddlers often enjoy the best of both worlds, appreciating both the calm of smaller groups and the energy of larger ones. A family get-together for Straddlers could include a mix of quiet areas for relaxation and spaces for group interaction. Planning activities that cater to both ends of the spectrum—such as a family trivia game followed by a group movie viewing—can be ideal for Straddlers.

Generationally, grandparents may appreciate events that honor family traditions or incorporate elements from their own childhood. Perhaps include activities or foods that have been passed down through the family, or encourage storytelling sessions where they can share their histories and experiences.

Remember to be considerate of their health and mobility needs, ensuring the venue is accessible and comfortable. Planning with empathy and understanding for their preferences will make these get togethers cherished occasions that celebrate the enduring bonds of family.

Walk Down Memory Lane with Them

Walking down memory lane with your grandparents can be a deeply enriching experience, allowing for a shared journey through their past, and creating a bridge to understanding and connection. It's an opportunity to honor their life stories and reinforce their sense of self, especially as they navigate the later chapters of their lives.

For CD grandparents, a quiet setting where they can share memories one-on-one or with a small group might be most comfortable. They might prefer looking through old photo albums, reading through letters, or visiting places of personal significance without the overstimulation of a large group.

MY grandparents may enjoy a more animated trip down memory lane. They might enjoy sharing their stories with a larger audience, perhaps during a family dinner or gathering, where they can recount their experiences with humor and gusto. Engaging with them through video recordings or storytelling sessions can allow them to express their vivacious personalities.

Straddlers will probably appreciate a balanced approach. They may enjoy a small family gathering where they can share stories with several generations present, perhaps while engaging in a mix of quiet reflection and more animated conversation.

When engaging in these memory-sharing experiences, it's important to consider generational differences. The contexts in which your grandparents grew up were likely very different from today's world, and their memories can provide invaluable insights into historical and personal family experiences. Use technology to your advantage; digitizing old photos or recording their stories can bridge the generational gap, allowing younger family members to access and appreciate these narratives.

It's crucial to be sensitive and respectful, as some memories may be emotional or difficult to share. Always lead with empathy and patience, allowing your grandparents to guide the journey at their pace and comfort level. This not only strengthens familial ties but also affirms the value of their life experiences and the wisdom they can impart.

Mail Them Letters

Mailing letters to your grandparents can be a heartwarming gesture of love and appreciation, and one that stands out in our digital age. The act of sending a handwritten letter can convey thoughtfulness and offer a personal touch that often gets lost in instant electronic communication.

For CD grandparents, who cherish their quiet time, receiving a letter can be a special event. They may appreciate the privacy and intimacy of reading a personal note that allows them to connect with you at their own pace. When writing to a CD grandparent, consider including personal reflections, anecdotes, or questions that invite them to write back when they feel inclined, fostering a deep and meaningful exchange.

MY grandparents, often the extroverts of the family, might love the surprise and display of affection that comes with receiving mail. They may enjoy letters that are lively and filled with news about family and friends, updates on your life, and funny or heartwarming stories. For MYs, consider enclosing photographs or drawings to make the letter more engaging, and perhaps even propose a playful pen-pal arrangement to keep the conversation bubbling.

Straddlers enjoy elements of both. A letter that mixes personal reflection with engaging storytelling can strike the right balance for them. They might appreciate a letter that invites a response but doesn't require one immediately, allowing them to savor the connection and respond in kind when they're ready.

In all cases, recognize the generational appeal of a letter. For many grandparents, letters were once the primary mode of long-distance communication, and revisiting this tradition can evoke a sense of nostalgia. Consider the tactile nature of letters; the feel of the paper, the sight of your handwriting, and even the stamp you choose can all contribute to making your grandparents feel special and remembered.

Regardless of personality type, mailing letters can bridge the physical distance between you and become cherished keepsakes that your grandparents can return to repeatedly, reminding them of your love and presence in their lives.

Make New Memories

Making new memories with grandparents isn't just about adding entries to a photo album, it's about creating experiences that enrich the bond between you. This pursuit is delightful yet nuanced, as it requires consideration of their personalities and preferences.

For CD grandparents, creating new memories could involve shared hobbies or interests. Perhaps it's starting a book club for two, where you read and discuss novels together, or working on a family history project where you can intertwine their past with your present. You could also engage in tranquil nature walks, where the serenity of the environment allows for deep conversations and peaceful silence alike.

MY grandparents might relish more dynamic and social activities. Organizing a surprise family reunion, attending a much-anticipated event together, or engaging in a group cooking session where recipes are both followed and improvised can be memorable. They may also enjoy learning a new skill with you, such as a dance class, which not only creates a memory but also develops a new shared hobby.

Straddlers, the ambiverts, might appreciate a balance of calm and excitement. A day trip to a new city, combining the thrill of exploration with the comfort of intimate conversations over coffee, could be ideal. They might also enjoy a crafting workshop where they can express themselves but still engage in a group setting, blending introspection with sociability.

Consider the evolving nature of memory-making, too. With younger generations, the activities might be more active or technology-oriented, such as playing a new video game together or starting a blog. With older generations, it might be about reliving past experiences with a modern twist, such as recreating a treasured family recipe with a new ingredient or technique.

Remember, making new memories isn't about the grandeur of the event but the quality of the experience. New memories lie in the laughter shared over a board game, the shared satisfaction of a project completed, or the warmth felt during a conversation about dreams and ideas. These memories become the threads that weave the tapestry of your family's history, imbuing it with color and warmth for years to come.

Help Them with Technology

Helping grandparents with technology is a practical way to show love and support, and it can significantly enhance their daily lives. For CDs, who may approach new technology cautiously or with a preference for solitude, one-on-one tutorials can be quite beneficial. Consider setting up a regular "tech day" where you patiently guide them through the functions of their devices. This could range from teaching them how to use a new smartphone app to showing them how to stream their favorite shows.

MYs often enjoy the social aspects technology can offer, so introducing them to platforms that connect them with others can be very rewarding. Help them set up a social media account to keep in touch with friends and family, or get them started on video calls to join in on family events they can't attend in person.

Straddlers may appreciate a blend of independence and guidance. They might enjoy trying out technology that requires some problem-solving but still allows them to feel a sense of accomplishment. Assist them in setting up smart home devices that can make daily tasks easier or introduce them to online workshops or classes that pique their interests.

Remember, the goal is to empower, not overwhelm. Start with the basics, proceed at a pace that suits their comfort level, and always be available for questions. Technology can often bridge the generational divide, allowing you to create shared experiences, such as playing online games together or collaborating on digital photo albums. This not only helps your grandparents stay current and connected but also provides a new avenue for interaction and memory-making.

Bring Them Thoughtful Gifts

Bringing thoughtful gifts to your grandparents can be a wonderful way to express your affection and show that you understand their likes, dislikes, and needs. Thoughtfulness is key, and the gift should resonate with their personality type.

For the CD, consider gifts that enhance their personal haven. A cozy blanket, a selection of teas, or a classic book can be perfect. They might also appreciate a puzzle or a craft kit that aligns with a hobby, offering them a peaceful way to spend time alone.

For the MY, choose something that acknowledges their outgoing nature and love for interaction. Tickets to a theater show, a gift certificate to a lively restaurant, or a subscription to a service that offers a variety of experiences could be ideal. They may also enjoy a personalized item that they can show off to friends, such as a custom-made piece of decor with a family crest or name.

Straddlers often like gifts that cater to both their introspective and social sides. For example, a journal that prompts reflection on various experiences or a gadget that can be used alone or with others, such as a new tablet pre-loaded with apps for reading and games, might be appreciated. Another option could be a board game that's fun to play solo or with family.

Remember to consider their life stage and any practical needs. For example, a magnifying glass with a light might be a considerate gift for someone who enjoys reading but struggles with small print. Or, for a grandparent who loves gardening but has mobility issues, an ergonomic gardening tool set could be helpful.

Gifts don't always have to be physical items. Sometimes, the best gift is your time and attention. For instance, creating a custom playlist of songs from their youth, organizing a family photo album, or even compiling a video montage of family messages can be deeply meaningful.

When selecting a gift, it's the thought and understanding of your grandparent's unique personality and preferences that counts. It's about showing that you know and appreciate who they are and that you cherish the relationship you have with them.

Offer to Help Them with Household Duties

Offering to help with household duties is a practical and compassionate way to show love to your grandparents, and ensures that their home environment remains a comfortable and safe space for them to enjoy. This gesture of support can be tailored to their individual personality types and physical capacities.

For the CD, who may value their independence and privacy, approach the subject gently. Offer to assist with tasks that are more physically demanding or time-consuming, such as yard work, organizing the garage, or deep cleaning. You might suggest doing these tasks together in a way that feels collaborative rather than intrusive.

The MY might appreciate a more direct and social approach. Offer to make a day of it, tackling a list of chores together followed by a meal or a fun activity. They could enjoy the companionship and the feeling of community effort. You could also consider setting up a regular schedule to help with chores, turning it into an opportunity for regular visits.

Straddlers may fluctuate in their openness to help, so offer options and let them guide you to the tasks they feel comfortable delegating. They might appreciate help with the more mundane tasks such as sorting bills, decluttering, or even setting up a system for managing everyday chores.

Remember to be mindful of their preferences and limitations. Some grandparents may be proud and not want to admit they need help, while others might fear losing their independence. It's important to be respectful, to listen, and to reassure them that your offer is born out of love and the desire to ensure they're living their best life.

Offering help with household duties is not just about physical help. It's also about spending quality time with your grandparents and showing that you care about their well-being. It's a tangible expression of your love and respect for them.

Key Takeaways

This chapter has delved into the art of fostering emotional closeness with grandparents while recognizing the distinct personalities of CDs, MYs, and Straddlers. It's a delicate balance of engagement, thoughtfulness, and respect for their individuality, ensuring that the emotional bond deepens with every shared moment.

- **Embrace Conversational Engagement:** Understand the importance of initiating dialogue tailored to different personality types—whether that be a CD's introspection or an MY's openness. It's about creating a space where every conversation feels purposeful and heartwarming.

- **Lead with Initiative:** Recognize the value in being the first to reach out, creating a proactive dynamic that honors your grandparent's personality, whether they're a Straddler or a CD. This shows that their presence is a priority in your life.

- **Personalize Surprise Gestures:** Craft moments of unexpected joy with gestures that resonate with their personality type, turning everyday surprises into treasured memories.

- **Design Inclusive Gatherings:** Plan family events with an understanding of how each personality type engages with family dynamics, ensuring grandparents feel a sense of belonging and joy in family milestones.

- **Foster Nostalgic Connections:** Share and create memories that honor your grandparents' life stories, whether they're reflective CDs or sociable MYs, enriching the familial tapestry with each shared recollection.

- **Keep Tradition Alive with Letters:** Send handwritten notes to bridge the generational divide, offering a tangible expression of affection that appeals to the sentimental side of all personality types.

- **Innovate Memory-Making:** Engage in activities that align with their energy and personality, whether it's a quiet hobby for a CD or a group activity for an MY, and craft new experiences that become the legacy of your shared time.

- **Demystify Technology Together:** Offer patient and personalized tech support, empowering your grandparents to connect and engage with the world in a way that's comfortable for their personality type.

- **Give with Thoughtfulness:** Select gifts that speak to their unique interests and life stage, showing that you value their individual tastes and experiences.

- **Lend a Helping Hand:** Provide help with daily tasks in a way that respects their independence and acknowledges their comfort levels, whether they are a self-sufficient CD or a sociable MY who enjoys the company.

Loving your grandparents is about embracing their uniqueness, cherishing their stories, and being present in the ways that matter most to them. By adopting the approaches outlined in this chapter, you pave the way for a richer, more fulfilling relationship with your grandparents—one that honors who they are and the legacy they carry.

Chapter Four

Celebrate Good Times

In the rich symphony of family life, grandparents are the resonant echoes of the past, embodying tradition and love in the present. However, as time goes on, the energy required to orchestrate celebrations can wane, leaving many grandparents on the quiet sidelines of festivity. This chapter focuses on rekindling the joy of celebrations, ensuring that the ones who once planned every detail are now guests of honor at life's banquet.

Whether it's transforming their space with the aroma of a home-cooked meal, taking the helm of family gatherings they can no longer manage, or marking the milestones of holidays and anniversaries with shared joy, each action is a testament to their lasting legacy.

In this chapter, we delve into the art of celebrating the grand tapestry of life with our elders—those who have sowed the seeds of our heritage. It's about recognizing the everyday alongside the extraordinary, thanking them for the foundations they laid, and ensuring that every "I love you" and every shared success or setback is an occasion in itself.

This chapter invites us to blend the old with the new, creating celebrations that are as timeless as they are timely, ensuring our grandparents remain at the heart of every cherished memory and new tradition forged. Through this journey, we aim to synchronize the rhythms of our lives with theirs, creating a harmonious melody that plays on, long after the music stops.

Go to Their Home and Cook for Them

Visiting a grandparent's home to prepare a meal is a deeply thoughtful act that caters to the individual preferences of CDs, MYs, and Straddlers alike. For the introverted CD grandparent, this gesture is a comfortable engagement, allowing them to enjoy companionship without the overstimulation of a crowded setting. It's an environment where subtle interactions take precedence, and quiet appreciation is the norm.

Conversely, for the extroverted MY grandparent, cooking serves as a catalyst for interaction and engagement. It is an opportunity for them to partake in lively conversation and to share stories, enriching the meal with personal narratives and shared laughter.

For the ambivert Straddler, such an occasion can be fine-tuned to involve them directly in the cooking process. This not only honors their knowledge and experience but also fosters a sense of partnership. It allows for an exchange of skills and storytelling, where both grandparent and grandchild can learn from each other.

When cooking for grandparents, the selection of dishes may often reflect dietary considerations and preferences, acknowledging the importance of health and comfort. It involves planning and preparing meals that are both nutritious and enjoyable, considering any dietary restrictions they may have.

This activity is not just about the food but also about the shared experience of preparing and eating it together. It's a demonstration of care that goes beyond the simple provision of sustenance, offering emotional nourishment and signifying a reciprocal relationship where the grandchild now offers care to the grandparent.

In summary, cooking for grandparents within their own home is a multi-faceted gesture. It respects the grandparent's autonomy and comfort zone, provides a shared activity that strengthens bonds, and acknowledges their contributions to the grandchild's life by reciprocating with a fundamental act of service.

Host Social Events or Gatherings

Hosting social events or gatherings in honor of grandparents recognizes the transition of roles in family dynamics, especially when they may feel too fatigued to organize such events themselves. This approach is respectful and empathetic, considering both the energy levels and the social appetites of CDs, MYs, and Straddlers.

For the CD grandparent, small, intimate gatherings are most suitable. These events should be low-key, with plenty of familiar faces to prevent them from becoming overwhelmed. It's a way of facilitating social interaction that respects their need for a controlled and calm environment.

On the other hand, the MY grandparent might appreciate larger, more animated gatherings. They draw energy from being around more people and partaking in robust conversations. Organizing an event with a diverse guest list can satisfy their love for social diversity and their desire to connect with a broader circle.

Straddlers, who possess traits of both CDs and MYs, may prefer a balanced event. A moderately sized gathering that allows for both group interactions and one-on-one conversations can cater to their fluctuating social preferences. Including activities that encourage participation without demanding constant social energy can be especially appealing.

In planning these events, it is crucial to manage the details, such as the event's duration, to avoid exhausting the grandparents. Ensuring they have a comfortable space to retreat to if they need a break is also considerate. The aim is to honor their lifetime of hosting by taking up the mantle in a way that acknowledges their current lifestyle and preferences.

Ultimately, hosting social events for grandparents is a celebratory and inclusive act. It allows them to enjoy the company of family and friends without the strain of organizing and managing the event, showing appreciation for their years of effort and providing them with joyful experiences in their later years.

Celebrate Important Holidays or Anniversaries Together

Celebrating important holidays or anniversaries together with grandparents is a meaningful way to honor the continuity of family traditions and create lasting memories. It's a gesture that underscores the value of their presence in the family's life and acknowledges the role they have played over the years.

For the CD grandparent, it's essential to recognize their preference for quieter, more reflective celebrations. Holidays and anniversaries can be commemorated with simple yet significant rituals that resonate with their sense of tradition and intimacy. A shared meal, a small family gathering, or a thoughtful conversation can be profoundly meaningful for them.

MY grandparents, who often relish festivities and larger social circles, might enjoy a grander celebration. Bringing together extended family members and friends, perhaps even incorporating elements of surprise, could make these occasions more joyful for them. A lively atmosphere with music, stories, and laughter can enliven their spirits and satisfy their social needs.

For Straddlers, a mix of both worlds is often the most rewarding. Combining an intimate family dinner with a more extensive get-together can give them the pleasure of deep personal connections and the enjoyment of a festive crowd. Offering them a role in planning or decision-making can also engage them, making them feel actively involved in the celebration.

Regardless of the grandparent's personality type, including them in the planning process can make them feel valued. Asking for their input on the celebration can ensure that the event aligns with their preferences and comfort levels.

It is important to consider not just the celebration itself but also the preparation and aftermath. Ensuring that grandparents are not burdened with responsibilities and can enjoy the festivities without stress is key.

Celebrating together fosters a sense of belonging and honors the shared history within a family. It's a reaffirmation of the grandparents' significance and a way to bridge generational gaps while creating new memories to cherish.

Create Hand-Made Gifts

Creating hand-made gifts for grandparents can convey a depth of sentiment that store-bought items may not. These gifts embody the time, creativity, and personal expression invested in their making, which can be special to the older generation.

For CDs, who often appreciate the thought and effort behind actions, a handmade gift can be a cherished token of personal connection. It's the uniqueness of the gift that speaks volumes, as it cannot be replicated or purchased, making it a symbol of the unique bond that you share. A hand-crafted photo album or a personalized story written just for them can be powerful gifts that resonate with their appreciation of depth and sincerity.

MY grandparents might relish the vibrancy and energy conveyed through a handmade gift. Something that reflects their interests or passions, such as a custom-painted flowerpot for a grandparent who loves gardening or a hand-knitted scarf in their favorite color, can spark joy and show an understanding of their personality. The liveliness of the gift, coupled with the personal touch, aligns with their love for expressive and memorable tokens of affection.

Straddlers might appreciate a balance between functionality and sentimentality in handmade gifts. An item that serves a practical purpose yet is infused with personal touches, such as a hand-crafted piece of furniture or a custom-made calendar with family photos, can be appealing. It shows thoughtfulness and consideration of their tastes and needs.

Handmade gifts can bridge the generational gap, allowing grandparents to feel the love and respect of their younger family members in a tangible form. These gifts can become heirlooms, carrying stories and memories from one generation to another. They stand as a testament to the time-honored tradition of giving something from the heart, something that the older generation can understand as a symbol of time well-spent and love genuinely expressed.

Here are some more specific handmade gift ideas tailored to different grandparents' personalities:

For CD Grandparents:

- A scrapbook or photo album chronicling special memories and milestones

- A playlist or CD of meaningful songs and artists from their era

- A personalized poetry book or collection of writings reflecting on your relationship

- A family tree illustration mapping out ancestral connections

- A quilted blanket or wall hanging made from scraps of old family clothing

For MY Grandparents:

- A customized recipe book of all their signature dishes

- A painted portrait or caricature capturing their lively spirit

- A video montage of family members sharing cherished memories

- A personalized jersey or trophy celebrating their interests and achievements

- A handmade coupon book for activities to enjoy together

For Straddler Grandparents:

- A handcrafted piece of furniture, jewelry box, or decorative item for their space

- A calendar filled with family photos marking special occasions

- A tech gadget such as a tablet or e-reader loaded with their favorite books/music

- A collection of handwritten letters bound into a book expressing what they mean to you

- A scrapbook time capsule with memorabilia from their life

The grandchild's personality type can also influence their approach. CDs may pour themselves into heartfelt, introspective gifts, MYs might create lively, visually engaging mementos, and Straddlers could strike a balance with practical yet personalized creations. The key is tailoring to both personalities while putting care into the meaning behind each gift.

Celebrate Them "Just Because"

Celebrating grandparents "just because" is a heartfelt way to show appreciation outside of traditional events and milestones. This shows an acknowledgement of their intrinsic value in our lives, outside of any particular achievements or occasions.

For CDs, this could mean choosing a random day to honor the quiet strength and consistent presence they embody. It could be as simple as arranging a visit to share a meal or taking a day trip to a place they enjoy, emphasizing the appreciation of their company. This approach highlights the importance of their role in the family dynamic, reinforcing their significance in daily life.

For MYs, a "just because" celebration might involve a spontaneous gathering of family and friends to highlight their social nature and love for community. A surprise party or an impromptu family game night that brings everyone together can be a joyous expression of gratitude for the energy and warmth they bring to the family.

Straddlers often appreciate a mix of personal attention and communal celebration. A "just because" occasion for them might include a personalized gesture, such as a heartfelt letter, coupled with a small family event. This combination honors their need for individual recognition and their role as a uniting force within the family.

These unscheduled celebrations can create lasting memories and foster a sense of your grandparents being valued for who they are outside of generic designated holidays. It's a spontaneous expression of love that can be deeply meaningful, reinforcing the message that their presence is a continuous source of joy and that every day with them is worth celebrating.

Thank Them for All That They've Done for You and Your Parents

Expressing gratitude to grandparents for their myriad contributions is a gesture that can deeply resonate with them. It's an affirmation of their enduring influence and the layers of support they've provided.

For CDs, who may appreciate quieter, more reflective acknowledgments, a bespoke gift such as a journal filled with family anecdotes, photos, and personal messages can be touching. In this journal, you could detail specific ways your grandparent has enriched your life, such as the time their wise counsel helped you navigate a personal dilemma or how their presence provided comfort during a difficult period. A page could be dedicated to a family story that exemplifies their role, for example, their methodical approach to problems that have taught you patience and resilience.

MYs, who often delight in expressive and communal appreciation, might enjoy a lively celebration in their honor. Organizing an event where family and friends can share stories of your grandparent's influence would be ideal. During this celebration, you could publicly recount times when their expansive energy and open-heartedness added vibrancy to family gatherings or how their bold spirit encouraged you to pursue your ambitions.

For Straddlers, who embody qualities of both CDs and MYs, a blend of private and public appreciation would be most suitable. Starting the day with a one-on-one activity, such as a shared hobby or a leisurely walk where you can express your gratitude in a personal setting, would be meaningful. This could be followed by a family event where everyone can articulate their thanks, sharing anecdotes that highlight their versatile influence, from the quiet support they provided behind the scenes to the more overt acts of love and guidance.

In each case, it's crucial to cite specific instances of support or wisdom that the grandparent has offered. Whether it was their guidance during key life decisions, the comfort of their recipes and traditions, or the lessons learned from their experiences, these acknowledgments illustrate the unique and profound impact they've had on your life.

This detailed appreciation not only honors their past contributions but also reinforces their ongoing significance in the family's life.

Remember Them on Father's Day and Mother's Day

Acknowledging grandparents on Father's Day and Mother's Day presents an invaluable opportunity to honor the unique contributions they've made to the family's lineage and the individual growth of its members. For the introspective CD grandparent, the celebration can be a subdued yet profound affair. A bespoke gift that reflects on shared experiences or interests, such as a first edition of a book they cherish or a framed photo of a cherished family memory, can speak volumes of your appreciation. Accompany this with a lengthy, heartfelt letter or a private reading of a piece of literature that resonates with your shared experiences, allowing them to revel in the quiet celebration of the bond you share.

In contrast, for the MY grandparent, a more public and vibrant celebration could be the highlight of their year. Organize a family-wide event, perhaps a virtual gathering if distances are a challenge, where each member recounts a tale or an anecdote that exemplifies their influence and vivacity. Enhance the occasion with a delivery of their favorite meal from a beloved restaurant or a cake from the family's preferred bakery, ensuring their taste for life's pleasures is indulged. You could also collaborate on a creative project, such as a family quilt or a scrapbook, with each family member contributing a patch or page that symbolizes their connection with the grandparent.

The key is to make these celebrations deeply personal and reflective of the grandparent's personality. For both CDs and MYs, it's about creating an experience that transcends the conventional, one that not only honors their role within the family but also reaffirms their individual legacy and the love that permeates through generations. Whether it's through quiet reflection or joyous festivity, the goal is to ensure that grandparents feel a profound sense of belonging and an acknowledgment of their irreplaceable impact on the family's fabric.

Recognize Their Achievements and Yours—Together

Recognizing the achievements of grandparents alongside your own creates a shared narrative of success and perseverance within the family, strengthening bonds and fostering mutual pride. For the CD grandparent, a one-on-one conversation can be a meaningful way to delve into these achievements. Discussing milestones over a shared activity that encourages introspection, such as assembling a puzzle or gardening, allows for a natural flow of conversation. You can reflect on the past and present accomplishments, drawing parallels between the challenges faced and overcome by both generations. It's an opportunity to express gratitude for the paths they've paved and the lessons their successes have imparted.

With the MY grandparent, consider a more exuberant celebration. Hosting a family gathering where everyone can highlight accomplishments with stories and toasts can be an engaging way to honor these moments. You might create a wall of fame displaying photographs, certificates, and mementos of shared achievements. During the event, encourage family members to share how the grandparent's accomplishments have inspired their own successes, emphasizing the generational ripple effect of their achievements.

Regardless of the approach, the focus should be on creating a sense of collective history and pride. It's about weaving the grandparent's achievements into the family's legacy and illustrating how their victories have laid the groundwork for your own. This shared recognition not only celebrates past successes but also inspires future aspirations, reinforcing the bond between grandparents and grandchildren, and honoring the intergenerational triumphs that form the family's story.

Tell Your Grandparents You Love Them

Expressing love to grandparents is a fundamental aspect of nurturing family connections, offering emotional support, and reinforcing the bonds between generations. For a CD grandparent, a heartfelt, simple statement of love can be profound. It may be best delivered in a quiet moment, perhaps during a shared activity that doesn't require eye contact, such as watching the sunset or while engaged in a hobby they love. This approach allows the sentiment to resonate in the space you share without the pressure of a direct confrontation, which can sometimes feel overwhelming for those who are more introverted.

When conveying love to an MY grandparent, consider a more direct and perhaps public expression. This might take the form of a heartfelt letter, a surprise visit, or a phone call just to say "I love you." For a grandparent who thrives on verbal affirmations and enjoys social interactions, these gestures will be deeply appreciated and can be a source of joy and pride.

For both CDs and MYs, regular expressions of love—be they through words, acts of service, or thoughtful gestures—reinforce the importance of their presence in your life. Remember, it's not just about the grandeur of the gesture, but the sincerity behind it. The aim is to make sure your grandparents feel valued and loved, understanding that they play an irreplaceable role in your life's narrative. Whether it's through daily check-ins, weekly visits, or personalized notes, these consistent affirmations of love contribute to their emotional well-being and strengthen the intergenerational fabric that binds your family together.

Share Life-Altering Moments with Them (Even the Bad Ones)

Sharing life-altering moments with grandparents is a crucial component of maintaining a strong, intergenerational bond. For CDs, who may prefer processing significant life events in a more introspective manner, it's important to share these moments in a way that is respectful of their space and temperament. A one-on-one conversation in a quiet setting can be the most appropriate method, where they have the opportunity to listen, reflect, and offer wisdom without the overstimulation of a group setting.

MYs might appreciate a more dynamic exchange. Sharing important news with them amidst a family gathering or through a video call where they can see your expressions and react in real-time might be more in line with their extroverted nature. They often thrive on being involved and expressing their thoughts and emotions openly.

Regardless of their disposition, keeping grandparents in the loop with both positive and negative developments conveys that their insight and presence are valued. It also allows them to provide support, celebrate successes, and offer comfort during challenges. Involving them in these moments is not just about sharing news, it's about reinforcing their role as mentors and confidants in the family's legacy. It's a mutual exchange where their experiences can guide you, and your shared experiences can bring new vitality to their lives.

By thoughtfully considering how to communicate these events to CD and MY grandparents, you ensure that the shared experiences are meaningful and that the emotional connections within the family continue to deepen and evolve.

Key Takeaways

This chapter has been a guide through the heartfelt process of integrating grandparents into our everyday lives and special moments, respecting and celebrating the unique dispositions of both CDs and MYs. It has underscored the importance of active and conscious grandparent-grandchild relationships that enrich the lives of both.

- **Embrace the Art of Personalization:** Tailor your interactions to suit the personalities of CD and MY grandparents. This careful attention ensures that the way you connect is both comfortable and enjoyable for them.

- **Celebrate Together:** Recognize and take part in celebrations of all scales, from grand festivities to the smallest of joys, fostering a sense of shared happiness and creating lasting memories.

- **Honor with Thoughtfulness:** Show gratitude for the past and present contributions of grandparents by creating personalized tokens of appreciation, such as handmade gifts, which carry a special significance.

- **Foster Emotional Expressiveness:** Encourage open declarations of love, ensuring that grandparents feel valued and emotionally connected to their grandchildren's lives.

- **Share the Spectrum of Life:** Confide in them during life-altering moments, allowing them to be a part of your journey through the highs and lows, thus deepening the familial bond.

- **Acknowledge Dual Contributions:** Celebrate achievements together, acknowledging the role grandparents have played in shaping the family's successes.

- **Maintain Tradition and Remembrance:** Keep grandparents in mind during significant days such as Father's Day and Mother's Day, as these gestures reinforce their importance within the family structure.

- **Show Appreciation:** Regularly express gratitude for grandparents' influence and support. This not only honors them but also models positive behavior for future generations.

By engaging with these key takeaways, you can cultivate a robust, intergenerational connection that honors the individuality of CD and MY grandparents. This connection not only enriches their lives but also serves as a powerful reminder of the familial tapestry to which they are indispensable. Through these actions, we weave a stronger, more compassionate family narrative that endures through generations.

Chapter Five

Appreciate Them

The intergenerational relationship between grandparents and grandchildren is a complex and rich one, often marked by an array of emotional dynamics. This chapter focuses on the importance of recognizing and appreciating the emotional strengths of our grandparents, while also acknowledging their humanity and the shared experiences that connect us. We'll examine the significance of engaging with them about their past, seeking their guidance on future decisions, and building a bond that goes beyond familial obligation. By fostering this deeper understanding and connection, we aim to encourage mutual respect and a more profound friendship. The goal is to not only identify and celebrate their contributions but also to integrate their insights into our lives, allowing for a reciprocal enrichment of perspectives.

Celebrate Their Emotional Strengths

Celebrating the emotional strengths of our grandparents is a powerful way to honor their role in our lives and acknowledge the wisdom they've accrued over a lifetime. This section delves into the various ways we can recognize and appreciate the unique emotional capabilities that our grandparents possess.

First, it's important to understand what constitutes emotional strength. For many in the older generation, these strengths may manifest as resilience built through decades of experiences, the capacity for deep empathy gained from diverse interpersonal interactions, or the ability to offer unwavering support and sage advice. These qualities often serve as the bedrock of our families, providing stability and guidance.

To celebrate these strengths, one can engage in heartfelt conversations, actively listen to stories of their past experiences, and reflect on the lessons these narratives hold. Expressing gratitude for their support, acknowledging the challenges they've overcome, and showing appreciation for their enduring presence in our lives are all gestures that can make a significant impact.

Moreover, documenting their stories, creating a family history project, or simply spending quality time discussing life's highs and lows can all be ways of honoring the emotional resilience and intelligence they bring to the family dynamic. By doing so, we not only pay tribute to their emotional strengths but also learn to cultivate these attributes within ourselves.

For CD grandparents, their inner resilience can be honored by setting aside quiet time together in a peaceful setting where they feel comfortable opening up to share stories of overcoming adversity throughout their lives. Create space for them to reflect on times when they demonstrated profound strength and perseverance in the face of life's difficulties. Their capacity for deep empathy can be celebrated through collaborative projects such as making a nostalgic memory book filled with old family photos. Spend time with them slowly

50 WAYS TO LOVE YOUR GRANDPARENTS 79

going through each photo, prompting them to share memories and reflecting together on the care and compassion they showed their loved ones in those moments.

For MY grandparents, their energetic enthusiasm for life can be celebrated by partaking in an active hobby or exercise routine together. Choose an activity that aligns with their zest for staying busy and engaged. Use the time together to express appreciation for their lively, spirited nature and how their passion for experiencing all life has to offer has touched you. Also, acknowledge their ability to motivate and inspire by sharing specific examples of how their stories of overcoming adversity gave you strength during your own challenging times. Tell them directly how their perseverance and good cheer in the face of hardship encouraged you to press on when things got difficult.

For Straddler grandparents, their adaptability can be honored by doing a variety of activities together that align with both their energetic and tranquil sides. Go on a peaceful nature walk together one day, using the quiet time to appreciate their versatility. On another day, you could play lively games that bring out their fun-loving spirit, highlighting their ability to adjust their energy levels to the situation. You can also celebrate their balanced perspective and skills as an advisor by sharing examples of how their practical wisdom helped guide you through important life decisions about relationships, careers, and other major choices. Express your gratitude for their ability to provide level-headed counsel that blends optimism with prudent caution.

Understand That They're Human—Just Like You

Acknowledging that our grandparents are human includes accepting their imperfections, understanding their limitations, and empathizing with their struggles. It's about seeing past the façade of the wise, unflappable elder, and looking to the individual who has lived through a spectrum of emotions and experiences.

For CDs, who may not always express their emotions openly, it's about respecting their need for space while quietly affirming their experiences. MYs, on the other hand, might share their humanity through stories and expressive conversations; here, active engagement and acknowledgment of their narratives are key. Straddlers, who embody traits of both, might appreciate a balanced approach of listening and sharing.

Understanding their humanity involves more than just intellectual acknowledgment; it requires action. It could mean offering support during difficult times, showing patience when they're set in their ways, or simply enjoying moments of laughter and joy together. It's about creating a space where they can be themselves without fear of judgment—a space where the unique bond between grandparent and grandchild can thrive.

For CD grandparents, their inward-focused nature may lead them to hide struggles related to declining physical health, feelings of loneliness, or fears about losing independence. Show empathy by accommodating their need for rest, initiating one-on-one visits, and reassuring them you will provide support when needed. Also, be aware of signs of depression such as withdrawal, and offer gentle encouragement to open up.

MY grandparents may express struggles, such as frustration over decreased mobility preventing social activities or grief over losing a spouse, more openly. Provide empathy through active listening without judgment, offering to accompany them on modified social outings, and providing comfort through shared memories. Be aware of the risk of isolation and make extra efforts to keep them engaged.

Straddler grandparents may fluctuate between silent suffering and vocal sharing depending on their mood. Check in frequently and learn to read their nonverbal cues indicating issues such as chronic pain or cognitive decline. Have open discussions about their preferences for support during vulnerable times. Adapt accordingly by being aware of when to provide comfort and when to give them personal space. The key is being attentive and letting them guide you on how to show empathy from moment to moment.

The most important thing with any grandparent is to not make assumptions. Create an environment where they feel safe opening up about their unique struggles. Offer support tailored to their needs, with the understanding that the aging process brings both shared and individual challenges. Show you acknowledge their humanity through patience, compassion, and respect.

Ask Them About Their Past

Exploring the past of our grandparents is a valuable approach to demonstrating our love and appreciation for them. When we invite them to share their stories and histories, we convey a sense of respect for their experiences and the paths they've walked. This section will delve into the nuances of this approach, tailored for CDs, MYs, and Straddlers.

For CDs, who might be more reserved, asking about their past can be a gentle invitation to open up at their own pace. It shows that we cherish their privacy yet are genuinely interested in their life stories. When they do share, it's important to listen intently, giving them the undivided attention they may quietly desire.

In contrast, MYs often relish the opportunity to recount their experiences. They feel loved and appreciated when their tales are met with enthusiasm and curiosity. Engaging with them through questions about their past reinforces their sense of belonging and the significance of their life's journey.

Straddlers might appreciate a mix of both listening and interactive conversation. They may share anecdotes spontaneously or reflect deeply when prompted. Showing interest in their past makes them feel valued as it honors both their reflective and expressive sides.

By asking our grandparents about their past, we are not just learning about their history—we are affirming their identity and the impact they have had on the world. This recognition can instill in them a profound sense of being loved and appreciated, as it celebrates their individuality and the legacy they will one day leave behind.

Understanding our grandparents' pasts is not just a matter of tracing family heritage; it's an exercise in recognizing the wealth of wisdom, resilience, and knowledge that they embody. It's important to show an interest in your grandparents' pasts to appreciate the rich tapestry of experiences that shape the wisdom they can impart to you and your family. Hearing about the pasts of your loved ones can be valuable for CDs, MYs, and Straddlers alike.

For CDs, the lived experiences of their grandparents can be like a treasure trove of quiet introspection. CDs often find solace in learning from the contemplative reflections of older generations, gaining insights that align with their inward-looking nature.

MYs may see their grandparents' past as a source of lively stories and a wellspring of lessons that they can apply in various social and personal contexts. Their enthusiasm for absorbing vibrant narratives can lead to a deeper understanding of their grandparents' resilience and adaptability.

Straddlers, who navigate both introspection and extroversion, can benefit from their grandparents' histories by finding balance in the wisdom gleaned. They can appreciate the stories as much for their informative content as for their emotional resonance, bridging the gap between knowledge and experience.

When we show interest in our grandparents' pasts, we signal that we value not only their presence in our lives but also the journey they've taken to get here. Their stories are not just tales of yesteryear; they're lessons in living, loving, and overcoming. By engaging with our grandparents about their history, we validate their experiences as essential building blocks of our own identity and understand that their lifetime of experiences can guide us through our own challenges. It's an acknowledgment that their legacy is interwoven with our present and future, creating a continuous thread of shared family wisdom.

Here are some sample questions tailored to each personality type to get grandparents sharing stories and experiences from their past:

For CD Grandparents:

- What is your favorite memory from childhood? I'd love to hear all about it.

- I'm curious, what was your relationship like with your parents?

- What is one of the most meaningful or important lessons you learned growing up?

- Can you tell me about what daily life was like for you as a child?

For MY Grandparents:

- Grandpa, what was the most exciting adventure from your youth? Please share all the details!

- Grandma, what were some of the fads and popular culture when you were a teenager?

- What were some of your fondest memories from attending school? Any favorite teachers or classes?

- What was dating and romance like back in your younger days? I'd love to hear your stories!

For Straddler Grandparents:

- What traditions or rituals from your childhood do you remember most fondly? Why were they so meaningful?

- Who were some of the most influential people in your life growing up? What impact did they have?

- What is a really powerful or poignant memory you have from your adolescence? I'd be grateful if you'd share it.

- What did you enjoy most about the place where you grew up? What did you find most challenging about it?

Ask Them for Advice on Your Future Endeavors

Asking grandparents for advice on future endeavors is an act that goes beyond seeking practical solutions; it's a meaningful gesture that affirms their significance in our lives and honors their accumulated wisdom. This section will elaborate on how involving grandparents in our decision-making processes can be beneficial for both parties and demonstrate how you can approach your grandparents for guidance, taking into account the preferences and communication styles of CDs, MYs, and Straddlers.

For CDs, who often deliberate deeply on their choices, grandparents can serve as a sounding board for their thoughtful considerations. Their advice can be especially valuable when it aligns with a CD's tendency toward careful analysis and measured steps. Encouraging CDs to solicit and reflect on their grandparents' insights can lead to enriched decision-making grounded in historical wisdom.

MYs might approach their grandparents with enthusiasm for their future plans, looking for advice that can help them navigate the broader social landscape. Grandparents can provide a unique perspective that tempers the MY's eagerness with the caution born of experience, offering anecdotes that are both instructive and inspiring.

Straddlers can benefit from their grandparents' advice by blending it with their own diverse set of approaches to problem-solving. They can harmonize the sagacity of their grandparents with their adaptive strategies, tailoring advice to fit a range of situations, thus benefiting from the best of both worlds.

In asking for advice, it's crucial to frame questions in a way that acknowledges the grandparents' expertise and experiences, showing that their contributions are valued and that their legacy extends into the future. This not only fosters a sense of usefulness and continued relevance in the grandparents but also provides a foundation of support and shared wisdom for the younger generation. Engaging in such dialogues can reinforce intergenerational bonds and ensure that the rich reservoir of knowledge and experience possessed by the older generation is passed on, respected, and applied.

Become Their Friend

Becoming friends with one's grandparents is a concept that reshapes traditional family dynamics, fostering a deeper and more egalitarian connection. This section of the book will explore practical ways to cultivate a friendship with grandparents, emphasizing mutual interests, shared experiences, and respect for their individuality, whether they are CDs, MYs, or Straddlers.

For CDs, building friendship may involve engaging in shared quiet activities, such as reading together or collaborating on a family history project. These activities allow for companionship without the pressure of constant conversation, respecting their need for space while fostering closeness.

MYs may enjoy more dynamic and social activities with their grandparents, such as attending community events or participating in a hobby class together. Through these shared experiences, MYs can connect with their grandparents in a vibrant and interactive way, celebrating their enthusiasm for life and the joy of discovery.

Straddlers, with their ability to adapt to various social settings, can alternate between quiet, introspective interactions and more lively, engaging activities. They might accompany their grandparents on a walk through nature one day and then join them in a spirited family game night the next.

To truly befriend grandparents, it's essential to communicate openly, showing genuine interest in their thoughts and feelings and sharing one's own in return. This reciprocal exchange transforms the relationship into one of mutual respect and camaraderie. It's about recognizing grandparents not just as elders but as individuals with rich personalities, stories, and a capacity for friendship that transcends generational divides.

By becoming their friend, one affirms the value of their grandparent's companionship and perspective, enriching both lives with the warmth and support that true friendship provides. This section will guide readers in nurturing this unique friendship, which can be as fulfilling and influential as any other in their lives.

Here are some suggestions for specific shared activities for friendship-building with each personality type:

For CD Grandparents:

- Work together on a genealogy project to trace your family roots and history. The quiet research time will suit their introverted nature.

- Attend a lecture on a topic of mutual interest at the local college or community center. The intellectual stimulation will appeal to their thoughtful side.

- Learn a new skill together such as painting or woodworking. The creative outlet can lead to rewarding one-on-one time.

For MY Grandparents:

- Join a low-impact exercise class that allows them to stay active and social. Bond over achieving fitness goals as workout buddies.

- Volunteer together at a charity event that supports a cause you both care about. Working side-by-side for the greater good can be deeply fulfilling.

- Take an interactive cooking class. Having fun while learning and making food memories can deepen your bond.

For Straddler Grandparents:

- Join a book club together. Reading the same book allows for insightful discussions.

- Take day trips to new places that offer a mix of calm sightseeing and stimulating new adventures.

- Develop a regular movie night with complimentary snack pairings and lively post-viewing discussions.

The key is finding activities that play to each grandparent's interests and temperament, so your quality time feels comfortable while also expanding your horizons together as friends.

Key Takeaways

This chapter has illuminated the various ways we can deepen our appreciation and understanding of our grandparents, recognizing their emotional strengths and embracing their humanity.

- **Celebrate Emotional Strengths:** Recognize and honor the emotional resilience and wisdom of grandparents. Whether they are CDs, MYs, or Straddlers, each has a unique emotional fabric that strengthens family ties.

- **Embrace Their Humanity:** Understand and empathize with the vulnerabilities and life experiences of grandparents. Acknowledge that, like us, they have traversed life's ups and downs and have a rich history to share.

- **Encourage Sharing of Past Experiences**: Invite grandparents to recount their past, thus affirming their life's journey and the wisdom they have to offer. This not only honors their experiences but also bridges generational gaps.

- **Seek Their Advice:** Value their insights on future endeavors. This not only taps into their vast reservoir of knowledge but also conveys respect for their judgment and experiences.

- **Cultivate Friendship:** Strive to build a friendship with grandparents that goes beyond familial roles. Engage with them in activities that resonate with their personality types, fostering a bond of mutual respect and enjoyment.

- **Respect Their Individuality:** Each grandparent will have their own preferences and personalities. Tailor your interactions to match their personality type, ensuring they feel comfortable and cherished.

- **Invest Time:** Dedicate time to be with your grandparents, showing that their company is desired and valuable. This investment of time is a clear indicator of love and appreciation.

- **Foster Open Communication:** Create a space where open and honest communication is the norm. Share your life with them and encourage them to do the same.

- **Support Their Interests:** Engage with and support the hobbies and interests of your grandparents. This shows that you care about their happiness and well-being.

- **Cherish the Moments:** Make the most of the time spent with grandparents. Each moment is an opportunity to strengthen your bond and create lasting memories.

By integrating these approaches into our relationships with our grandparents, we demonstrate profound love and respect for them. This chapter provides the tools to not only express our affection but to also solidify a robust, intergenerational connection that enriches both our lives and theirs.

Chapter Six

Boundaries

Establishing and respecting boundaries is an essential component of any healthy relationship, and this remains true in the grandparent-grandchild dynamic. This chapter delves into the delicate art of setting boundaries with our grandparents while maintaining respect and affection. It's about recognizing their role and wisdom in our lives while also asserting our own needs and expectations. As we explore the balance between guidance and autonomy, we'll discuss how to appreciate their advice, navigate misunderstandings with empathy, and ensure that our language and actions reflect respect. We'll also touch upon the importance of personal time, reinforcing that while our relationship with our grandparents is treasured, our individual well-being is just as crucial. Understanding these boundaries is key to nurturing a relationship that is both loving and mutually respectful.

Set Boundaries for Your Grandparents

Setting boundaries with grandparents is a careful process that involves clear communication and mutual respect. It's essential to articulate personal limits in a way that honors the relationship while preserving one's own space and autonomy.

For grandparents who are CDs, a straightforward and direct approach is often appreciated, as they tend to value privacy themselves. A simple conversation about your needs and when you are available can help set clear expectations without causing offense.

With MY grandparents, who may enjoy more interaction, it's important to acknowledge their desire for connection while gently establishing when and how often you can engage in activities or conversations. Offer alternatives that suit both of your schedules.

For Straddlers, a blend of these tactics works best, adapting to their fluctuating need for interaction and solitude.

Setting boundaries is not just about saying no, it's about creating a framework for a relationship that allows for mutual respect and understanding. This includes being honest about your feelings, being consistent in your actions, and respecting their boundaries in return.

When done thoughtfully, setting boundaries strengthens relationships, ensuring that both you and your grandparents feel loved and appreciated without feeling overwhelmed or disregarded. It's a delicate balance that, when maintained, leads to a healthy and enduring bond.

Examples of boundaries may include:

- **Visitation Boundaries:** It's important to establish specific days and times for visits to ensure that neither party feels overwhelmed or taken for granted. This respects the grandparent's need for company and the grandchild's need for personal space.

- **Communication Boundaries:** Decide on appropriate times for phone calls or video chats, especially if there's a difference in routines or time zones.

- **Emotional Boundaries:** Be open about topics that are comfortable for discussion, thereby avoiding any potential discomfort or emotional distress.

- **Physical Space Boundaries:** If living together, agreeing upon shared and private spaces within the home can help maintain independence and comfort for both parties.

- **Decision-Making Boundaries:** It's vital to respect each other's right to make personal decisions without unsolicited advice or interference.

- **Financial Boundaries:** Set clear guidelines about financial support or gifts to prevent any misunderstanding or strain on the relationship.

Boundaries are needed to ensure that the relationship remains positive and doesn't become a source of stress or resentment. They help in managing expectations and fostering a sense of mutual respect. For example, a grandparent might need to understand that a grandchild has their own life and responsibilities, which means they can't always be available at a moment's notice. Conversely, a grandchild needs to recognize that grandparents might have their own set of limitations or routines that need to be acknowledged.

Here are some examples of how to initiate boundary-setting conversations tailored to each personality type along with sample dialogues:

For CD Grandparents:

"Grandma, I wanted to talk about our visit schedules. I love spending time with you, but my work schedule makes it hard for me to drive out more than once a week. Can we set a standing Sunday visit so I can plan my week? I'd also feel more comfortable calling before I head over just to be sure it's a good time."

For MY Grandparents:

"Grandpa, I know you love when I'm able to call and chat, but with the kids and work, it's hard for me to connect as often as I'd like. Would it work for us to set up a standing call once or twice a week when the kids are occupied? I want to make sure I'm able to give you my full attention. The same goes for visits. If we can plan those in advance, I can be sure to be free of other commitments."

For Straddler Grandparents:

"Nana, I cherish our walks together, but I'm struggling to manage my energy levels lately with work and family needs. Could we limit our walks to once or twice a week? I don't want to lose our special time together, but I need to be realistic. I'm happy to bring the kids to visit you more often at home, too. Let's chat about what routine would work well for both of us."

The key is in clearly communicating your own limitations while reassuring them of your love and desire to spend time together. Setting a predictable routine can allow for better planning and prevent hurt feelings.

Ask for Advice and Listen When They Give It

Grandparents are repositories of experience and wisdom, having navigated many of life's challenges. Engaging with them for advice is not only a gesture of respect but an opportunity to gain insights that are often not available in textbooks or online resources. When you ask your grandparents for advice, you acknowledge the value of their life experiences and offer them a sense of involvement in your life.

For CDs, who may rarely share their thoughts unless prompted, asking for advice can encourage them to open up and share their rich inner thoughts. It shows that their perspective is valued and that their quiet observation over the years is recognized as a source of wisdom.

MYs, who typically enjoy sharing their opinions, will appreciate the opportunity to express their thoughts and feel that their experiences can serve a meaningful purpose in guiding you. Asking for their advice is a way to validate their life's journey and the knowledge they've accumulated.

Straddlers, who oscillate between the two extremes, can offer a balanced viewpoint, drawing upon a mix of introspection and outward experience. Asking for their advice and actively listening can tap into this equilibrium of wisdom.

When they impart their advice, listening is just as important as asking. It's crucial to give them your full attention, reflect on what they say, and acknowledge their input even if you decide to take a different path. This communicates that you respect them and value their contributions to your decision-making process.

By incorporating their guidance into your future endeavors, you not only benefit from your grandparents' knowledge but also foster a deeper connection with them. It's a way of letting them know they play an important role in your life and that their legacy of wisdom continues through you. This can be a profound way of showing love and respect, making them feel cherished and relevant.

Give Them the Benefit of the Doubt During Misunderstandings and Understand They're from a Different Time

Misunderstandings can arise in any relationship, and when they occur with grandparents, it's essential to approach the situation with patience and understanding. Given the generational gap, there will be times when worldviews clash or communication breaks down. It's important to give grandparents the benefit of the doubt during these moments, recognizing that they come from a different time with different social norms and life experiences.

For CDs, who may retreat into silence during a misunderstanding, it's crucial to gently encourage dialogue and express a willingness to understand their perspective. This approach allows you to find common ground and resolve issues without pressure.

MYs might vocalize their confusion or disagreement more openly. Listen actively and validate their feelings while calmly sharing your viewpoint. This can help bridge the gap between different eras and perspectives, fostering mutual respect.

Straddlers might fluctuate in their response to misunderstandings. They might withdraw at times or be outspoken at others. Offering them understanding and a non-judgmental space to express themselves can lead to a more balanced resolution.

Understanding that your grandparents are from a different time involves acknowledging the vast array of experiences that have shaped their beliefs and behaviors. It's about respecting their journey through life and the societal context they've lived in. When you approach misunderstandings with empathy and give them the benefit of the doubt, you help to create a forgiving and supportive environment. This kindness can make them feel loved and appreciated, despite the inevitable challenges that come with the evolving social landscape.

Here are some examples of historical and cultural differences that can lead to misunderstandings between generations:

- **Gender Roles and Expectations:** Grandparents may have more traditional views on appropriate behavior, activities, or careers for men and women. These can clash with modern egalitarian attitudes.

- **Parenting Styles:** Previous generations often had more authoritarian styles of parenting emphasizing strict discipline. This can contrast with newer models focused on emotional nurturing and open communication.

- **Societal Norms:** Taboos around topics such as sex, mental health, and substance abuse have eased over time. Grandparents may be uncomfortable discussing issues that seem routine to younger generations.

- **Race Relations:** While progress has been made, grandparents grew up in times of more overt racism and segregation. Their perspectives may seem antiquated or prejudiced through a modern lens.

- **Technology Use:** Younger people have grown up immersed in technology. Grandparents may struggle to understand new gadgets or social media. Different views on screen time for kids can also emerge.

- **Work Ethic:** Older generations often emphasize diligence and "paying your dues" in a career. Younger people may focus more on work-life balance and fulfillment.

- **Political Perspectives:** Sociopolitical dynamics have evolved drastically in recent decades. Grandparents' stances may appear old-fashioned or rigid to more progressive youth.

Bridging these gaps requires empathy, patience, and compromise. Recognizing how cultural shifts impact perspectives can help address conflicts respectfully when cross-generational differences surface.

Avoid Being Offensive with Your Language

Language is a powerful tool that can either bridge gaps or create barriers. When interacting with grandparents, it's pivotal to be mindful of language, ensuring it is respectful and considerate. This is not merely about avoiding swear words or slang that might be unfamiliar or uncomfortable for them but is also about steering clear of statements that may unintentionally dismiss or belittle their beliefs, experiences, or emotions.

For CDs, who may already be hesitant to engage in lengthy conversations, using harsh or offensive language can further alienate them. Instead, choose words that are gentle and inclusive, which can encourage them to open up and contribute to the conversation.

MYs may respond to offensive language with hurt or even confrontational retorts. They often appreciate direct communication but still require that it be delivered with tact and respect. Ensuring your words are considerate can keep discussions open and lively without crossing into disrespect.

Straddlers might be adaptable in conversation, but like anyone, they deserve communication free from offense. They appreciate a balanced approach where language is used thoughtfully, reflecting a blend of openness and politeness.

Being careful with your language shows a deep level of respect and consideration for your grandparents' feelings and values. It contributes to a positive, nurturing environment where they can feel safe and valued. This attentiveness to language affirms their worth and dignity, promoting a relationship built on understanding and mutual respect. It's a simple yet profound way to honor their identity and experiences, showing that they are cherished members of the family.

Here are some examples of potentially offensive language to avoid and more respectful alternatives when interacting with grandparents:

Avoid:

- **Profanity:** Be mindful of strong swear words, which may be upsetting or seem disrespectful.

- **Dismissive Language:** Don't use phrases such as "you don't understand" or "that makes no sense." This can come across as patronizing.

- **Mocking Tone:** Even light sarcasm or mimicry can feel hurtful. Remember, your words carry weight.

- **Sensitive Topics:** Risqué jokes about sex, bodily functions, etc. may make your grandparents uncomfortable. Tread lightly.

- **Deprecating Humor:** Teasing that seems harmless to you may feel like a personal attack to your grandparents. Err on the side of tact.

Use Instead:

- **A Gentle Tone:** Keep your tone warm and polite even when disagreeing. This puts your grandparents at ease.

- **Validation:** Affirm your grandparents' thoughts and opinions before politely sharing your own. This shows respect.

- **Clarifying Questions:** If confused, ask for clarification without judgment. Maintain curiosity.

- **Encouraging Phrases:** "I appreciate you sharing that..." "I hadn't considered that point of view." This supports open dialogue.

- **Mindful Wording:** Avoid language that generalizes or stereotypes. Be precise and thoughtful.

With some self-awareness and care, we can select words that honor our grandparents as beloved elders deserving of dignity. A little mindfulness goes a long way.

Don't Forget "You" Time

Maintaining a balanced relationship with grandparents includes ensuring personal time for self-care and independent pursuits. "You" time is not just a luxury, it's a necessity for emotional and mental well-being. It allows for the recharge of one's batteries and fosters a sense of individuality that is healthy for all relational dynamics.

For CDs, personal time is crucial. It's their sanctuary for introspection and rejuvenation. Respecting this need for solitude is key, as it allows them to be fully present during times of family interaction.

MYs may thrive on engagement, but they too benefit from "you" time, which might involve solo activities that are energizing and reflect personal interests. For MY grandchildren, this time apart can enhance their appreciation for shared moments with grandparents.

Straddlers navigate between the need for social interaction and solitude. Balancing "you" time for them means allocating enough space to enjoy both their private and social sides without neglecting either.

Encouraging and respecting "you" time within the family structure underscores the importance of personal space and self-care. It's about recognizing the individual needs of each family member and ensuring that everyone's mental and emotional tanks are well-filled. This practice sets a powerful example for grandparents, who also need to be reminded of the importance of maintaining their own hobbies and interests. By prioritizing themselves, each member of the family can come together with renewed spirits, ready to engage and support one another in a more meaningful way.

Here are some tips for communicating the need for personal time while reassuring grandparents of their importance, along with self-care activity ideas:

Tips for Communicating:

- Acknowledge how much you cherish your time together and how important your grandparents are to you before bringing up needing personal time. This cushions the conversation.

- Explain that you are feeling overwhelmed/drained and need to prioritize self-care to be fully present when you are together. Frame it as benefiting your relationship.

- Suggest specific alternative visiting days/times that could work well so they don't feel fully rejected. Compromise.

- Share your plans for your personal time—explain that you are pursuing hobbies or seeing friends. This reduces any fears that you're isolating your grandparents.

- Promise to check in with them and be responsive if urgent needs arise during your "you" time. Reassure them.

Self-Care Activity Ideas:

- Read books, draw/paint, or explore hobbies such as photography, crafting, gardening, and meditation.

- Exercise, for example, yoga, hiking, biking—anything that gets you moving.

- Pamper yourself with a bath, facial, massage, or pedicure.

- See a movie, go to a museum/show, and enjoy nature.

- Meet friends for meaningful connection and laughter.
- Prioritize your health—get your teeth cleaned or go for a massage.

With open communication, flexibility, and self-awareness, you can balance your grandparents' need for companionship with your own need for replenishment.

Key Takeaways

As we close this chapter, we crystallize the essence of fostering harmonious relationships with grandparents, recognizing the distinct generational differences and personality types of CDs, MYs, and Straddlers. This chapter has been a guide to navigating these waters with grace and understanding.

- **Embrace Generational Wisdom:** Acknowledge the wealth of knowledge and experience grandparents bring to the family dynamic. Valuing their advice bridges the generational gap and enriches the family's collective wisdom.

- **Set Respectful Boundaries:** Establishing clear and considerate boundaries is essential for a healthy relationship. It shows mutual respect and creates a comfortable space for all family members to coexist.

- **Nurture Open Communication:** Cultivating an environment where open dialogue is encouraged allows for a deeper understanding and prevents misconceptions. It's the bedrock of trust and empathy within the family.

- **Practice Language Sensitivity:** Being mindful of language emphasizes the importance of respect and kindness in family interactions. It avoids unintended harm and fosters a positive atmosphere.

- **Preserve Personal Time:** Upholding the necessity for "you" time ensures that each family member remains grounded in their identity and well-being. It's about striking the right balance between family obligations and self-care.

- **Leverage the Benefit of the Doubt:** Employing this principle during misunderstandings mitigates conflicts and promotes a culture of forgiveness and patience within the family.

- **Cultivate Mutual Understanding:** Encourage a bi-directional learning process where both younger and older generations take the time to understand each other's perspectives, leading to a more cohesive family unit.

- **Demonstrate Flexibility and Adaptability:** Show that family members are willing to adjust their expectations and behaviors to accommodate each other's comfort levels, enhancing family harmony.

- **Value Individuality and Togetherness:** Recognize that while each person has their unique traits and needs, the strength of the family lies in its unity and the shared experiences that bind.

- **Model Empathy and Compassion:** Set an example by treating grandparents with empathy and compassion, illustrating the family's core values and teaching by example.

Implementing these key takeaways not only solidifies the bond between grandchildren and grandparents but also fortifies the family's foundation, making it resilient to the nuances of time and change. The chapter aims to equip families with the tools to cherish the old, embrace the new, and blend the best of both worlds for a fulfilling and enriched family life.

Chapter Seven

Socializing with Your Grandparents as an Adult

In the ever-evolving landscape of family relationships, the bond between adults and their grandparents remains a cornerstone of heritage and wisdom. This chapter turns the pages back to the roots, where the old and the new generations meet. It's a journey, intertwining the past with the present and embracing the lessons and legacies that our grandparents embody. As adults, the approach to socializing with our elders pivots from mere familial obligation to a cherished opportunity for growth and connection. Here, we explore the avenues to not only maintain but also enrich these ties. By integrating consistent communication, shared experiences, and mutual respect into our routines, we build bridges across generations. The fabric of family is strengthened through each call, each hug, and every shared holiday, weaving a tapestry of memories and understanding. This chapter aims to guide you through the nuances of these interactions, ensuring that as the years progress, the connection with your grandparents deepens and is rooted in love, appreciation, and the acknowledgment of their pivotal role in the family saga.

Call Them Often

Regular communication is the lifeline of any relationship, and this is particularly true for the bond with your grandparents. In a world where time is often a scarce commodity, making the effort to call your grandparents frequently is a testament to their importance in your life.

Grandparents, having witnessed the passage of many seasons, often place immense value on the currency of time and the act of sharing it. Your call can be a bridge across the generational divide, an affirmation of their relevance, and a celebration of their continued presence in your life.

- **Set a Schedule:** Establish a routine that fits both your schedule and theirs. Whether it's a specific day of the week or a particular time of day, consistency creates anticipation and joy.

- **Be Present:** In the moments you share over the phone, ensure you're fully present. Listen actively and engage genuinely. The quality of the conversation often matters more than the quantity.

- **Share Your World:** Update them on your life and seek their input on decisions or experiences. This inclusion reinforces their role as a valued member of your family.

- **Ask About Their Lives:** Show interest in their activities, health, and feelings. Your concern for their well-being demonstrates that they are loved and not alone.

- **Use Technology to Your Advantage:** If they're comfortable with technology, consider using video calls or sharing photos and videos through messaging to keep in touch. Using technology can make conversations more personal and engaging.

- **Be Adaptive:** Sometimes, a call may not be convenient. Be flexible and considerate of their needs and preferences and consider supplementing phone calls with handwritten letters or postcards.

By calling your grandparents often, you weave a pattern of care and connection that enriches both of your lives. It's a simple yet profound gesture that acknowledges the significance of your shared history and the depth of your familial bonds.

Ask Them How They Are at Least Once a Week

Establishing a routine of communication with grandparents is pivotal, regardless of their personality type. A weekly check-in serves as a touchstone for connection and understanding, allowing each grandparent to share their world with you.

For the MY grandparent, this interaction is a source of joy and anticipation. They eagerly await the chance to recount their experiences and express their thoughts. During these conversations, it's crucial to offer them the space to articulate their feelings and share their week's adventures. They may regale you with stories, seek your opinions on various matters, or simply revel in the familial bond that these conversations strengthen.

In contrast, CD grandparents might approach these weekly calls with a more reserved demeanor. They value consistency and the knowledge that you care, even if they don't always have much to say. The act itself is comforting. Your task is to gently coax them into sharing, respecting their pace and their preference for listening rather than speaking. Showing interest in their quiet pursuits can encourage them to open up over time.

Straddler grandparents often fluctuate between these two modes. They appreciate the regularity of the conversations but may vary in their level of engagement from week to week. Recognizing and responding to their conversational cues is key. Some weeks they may have a lot to share, mirroring the MY's enthusiasm, while at other times, they may prefer a more listening role like the CD.

These weekly check-ins should be more than mere updates; they are opportunities to delve deeper into their emotional and mental well-being. Asking open-ended questions can unearth concerns or joys that might otherwise remain unspoken. It's also a moment to reassure your grandparents of their importance in your life and to reinforce that they are not alone, whatever their temperament or situation.

Additionally, this regular communication is not just a monologue but a dialogue. Sharing your own life updates can help maintain a balanced relationship. It allows your grandparents to feel they are still a part of your life's tapestry, offering them a chance to provide guidance, share in your triumphs, or offer support during challenges.

In the end, these weekly conversations are a fundamental practice in expressing love and respect for your grandparents, recognizing their individuality, and ensuring they remain an integral part of the family's narrative. It's about creating a reliable rhythm in their lives where they feel heard, seen, and deeply valued.

Hug Them

In the realm of human interaction, physical touch holds a language of its own, capable of conveying warmth, safety, and love without a single word spoken. Hugging your grandparents embodies these sentiments, providing a tangible expression of your affection and connection. It transcends the barriers of age and words, allowing for a heartfelt exchange between adult grandchildren and their grandparents.

For MY grandparents, a hug is an exuberant celebration of your relationship. It's an open invitation for them to share joy and energy and to feel the vibrancy of the family bond in a physical form. They often receive hugs as a testament to their cherished role in the family and may respond with equal enthusiasm, offering a robust embrace that resonates with their extroverted spirit.

Conversely, CD grandparents might approach physical affection with a degree of reservation. A hug for them is a quiet yet profound acknowledgment of the bond you share. It must be offered with sensitivity, respecting their comfort zone while also affirming your presence and care. A gentle, reassuring hug can communicate volumes to a CD grandparent, serving as a silent affirmation of your enduring bond.

Straddler grandparents can vary in their response to physical touch. Sometimes they may lean into a hug with the same fervor as an MY, while at other times they might accept it with the serene contentment of a CD. The key with Straddlers is to read their current mood and match their level of engagement, ensuring that the hug feels genuine and comfortable for both of you.

Incorporating hugs into your social interactions with grandparents as an adult is not merely about the act itself; it's about the intention and emotion that the gesture carries. It's a recognition of their significance in your life and an acknowledgment of the shared history and affection. It's also an affirmation of their need for closeness and physical presence in a world that often becomes less tactile for older adults.

A hug can be especially poignant during life's transitions or moments of celebration, serving as a mutual source of comfort and happiness. It's a reminder that, despite the inevitable changes that come with time, the physical bond between you and your grandparents remains unchanged.

Hugging your grandparents should be a conscious, considerate act—never rushed; always sincere. It's an embrace that says, "You are important to me, and I cherish our connection," sealing the sentiment in a moment of shared warmth.

Get Together for the Holidays

The tapestry of family life is often most vividly colored during holiday gatherings, where the spirit of tradition and celebration weaves connects family members from different generations. For adult grandchildren, these occasions offer a precious opportunity to strengthen the bonds with their grandparents, partake in shared rituals, and create lasting memories.

For MY grandparents, holidays are a stage for exuberance and connection. These events are often eagerly anticipated, as they provide a platform for storytelling, laughter, and communal joy. When planning holiday gatherings, include activities that cater to their love of engagement and communication. Encourage them to regale the family with tales of past holidays or lead a cherished family tradition. Their extroverted nature will revel in the holiday's collective spirit, making them feel integral to the festivities.

CD grandparents might appreciate a more subdued holiday observance. They find solace in the quieter aspects of gatherings—perhaps a serene moment shared over a cup of tea or a reflective conversation beside the fire. Intimate, peaceful moments where they can connect with family members individually often mean more to them than the grandeur of a festive party. For these grandparents, the holidays are a time to reinforce the familial fabric with gentle stitches, quietly reinforcing the binding ties.

Straddler grandparents often enjoy a blend of both worlds. They may oscillate between leading a lively holiday game and retreating to a corner for a heartfelt one-on-one conversation. With them, it is vital to offer a holiday experience that allows for both social excitement and personal interaction. Balancing the day's schedule to include group activities and quieter periods can help Straddlers feel content and connected.

Regardless of their personality type, getting together for the holidays is a gesture that underscores the importance of your grandparents in the family hierarchy. It is a reaffirmation of their legacy and the values they have instilled across generations. These occasions are a time for gratitude and reflection and offer an opportunity to nurture the familial bond.

When planning holiday get-togethers, consider the accessibility and comfort of your grandparents. Ensure that they are actively included in the planning process and that their needs and preferences are accounted for. Whether it's facilitating travel arrangements or preparing their favorite dish, these considerations demonstrate respect and thoughtfulness.

In the end, the act of gathering for the holidays is a profound expression of love and respect for your grandparents. It is an acknowledgment of their enduring presence and influence in your life. Through the shared joys and rituals of the season, you not only honor the traditions of the past but also lay the groundwork for future memories, ensuring that the holiday spirit continues to flourish within the heart of the family.

Let Them Spend Time with Your Kids and Partner

Allowing grandparents to spend time with your children and partner serves as a bridge between generations and cements family relationships. These interactions present a chance for your grandparents to impart wisdom, share experiences, and build individual bonds that enrich the family's social fabric.

For MY grandparents, this time can be filled with activity and conversation. They might relish taking the grandchildren to parks or museums, engaging in spirited discussions at the dinner table, or organizing family outings that include everyone. These experiences enable them to share their zest for life and to play an active, participatory role in the lives of younger family members.

CD grandparents may prefer quieter, more intimate settings to connect with your children and partner. Reading stories to the grandchildren, helping with homework, or engaging in one-on-one conversations allows them to bond in a manner that respects their need for tranquility and depth of interaction.

Straddler grandparents can adapt to various social situations, comfortably oscillating between active engagement and calm moments. They might teach your children a skill or hobby and later enjoy a more low-key activity such as watching a movie or playing a board game. Their ability to shift between different modes of interaction makes them versatile companions for your children and partner.

Incorporating your partner into these dynamics is equally important. It can be through shared responsibilities, such as preparing a family meal together, or through recreational activities that all can enjoy. This shared time is an opportunity for your partner to understand your family's history and for your grandparents to appreciate the new dimensions your partner brings to the family.

Remember, the goal of these interactions isn't just to fill time but to create meaningful connections and memories. While it's beneficial to have structured activities, it's also important to allow for organic, unstructured time where relationships can grow naturally.

Facilitating these interactions requires consideration of everyone's comfort levels and interests. It involves being attentive to the needs and limits of all parties, ensuring that the time spent together is enjoyable and stress-free.

By fostering these multigenerational relationships, you not only honor your grandparents but also provide your children and partner with a richer sense of family continuity and belonging.

Treat Them to Dinner or Ice Cream

Treating grandparents to dinner or ice cream is more than a simple act of taking them out for a meal; it is a gesture that nourishes your relationship through shared experiences and creating moments of joy. This is an opportunity to step into their world, indulge in their preferences, and make them feel special and valued.

For MY grandparents, a dinner outing can be an event filled with lively conversations and laughter. Choose a vibrant eatery that resonates with their sociable nature where the atmosphere is as enriching as the food. Following dinner with ice cream could turn into a spontaneous adventure—perhaps you could try out the new dessert parlor they've been curious about or enjoy a walk in the park with a cone in hand.

CD grandparents may appreciate a more serene dinner environment where the ambiance allows for deeper conversations and a relaxed pace. A quiet restaurant that offers a sense of privacy would be ideal, and for dessert, a peaceful spot where you can sit and savor ice cream together would be perfect for them.

Straddler grandparents can enjoy the best of both worlds. A dinner that starts in a calm setting and gradually moves to a more dynamic environment for dessert could suit their flexible nature. Perhaps begin with a meal at their favorite restaurant and then venture to a popular ice cream shop where they can engage with the surroundings at their own pace.

When you treat your grandparents to dinner or ice cream, it's not just about the food but the quality of the time spent together. It's about being present, engaging with them, and listening. Through sharing a meal, you provide opportunities for stories to be shared and wisdom to be imparted, and you show your grandparents that their company is a pleasure in your life.

Ensure that the choice of venue and the timing are considerate of their preferences and health needs. The act should be effortless, allowing them to enjoy the experience without worry or discomfort. It's about creating a space where they feel cherished and where the simple pleasure of a meal or a sweet treat becomes a memorable event that strengthens your bond.

Experience New Activities or Hobbies Together

Inviting grandparents to share in new activities or hobbies is a way to strengthen intergenerational connections and foster mutual learning. This initiative isn't just about the activity itself; it's a channel through which you can share enthusiasm, curiosity, and growth, creating new memories in the process.

For MY grandparents, who thrive on engagement and energy, consider activities that are social and stimulating. Think of a dance class that invites laughter and movement, or a cooking workshop where they can interact and express their zest for life. Choose hobbies that allow them to shine, share stories, and immerse themselves in the joy of the moment with others.

CD grandparents may prefer activities that are more introspective or subdued. This could be a craft workshop, where the focus is on the meticulous joy of creation, or perhaps bird watching, which offers a tranquil connection with nature. Engaging in these activities together provides a serene space for conversation and bonding at a comfortable pace.

For Straddler grandparents, a blend of tranquility and engagement would be ideal. A gardening project, for example, can be both meditative and social, allowing them to switch between introspection and interaction. Another option could be a book club that meets occasionally, combining the solitary pleasure of reading with the communal joy of discussion.

When experiencing new activities or hobbies together, it's important to be attentive to your grandparents' abilities and interests. The goal is to ensure that the experience is enjoyable and not overwhelming. It's not about pushing them into the unknown but guiding them into experiences that can be enriching and enjoyable.

This shared exploration is a two-way street; it's about you stepping into their world of experience and wisdom, and them stepping into yours filled with new perspectives and possibilities. It's a chance to learn from each other, to grow together, and to appreciate each other's company in new and dynamic ways. The novelty of the experience can be thrilling, but it's the shared journey of discovery that truly cements the bond.

Take Them on a Multi-Generation Family Vacation

Taking grandparents on a multi-generational family vacation offers a unique opportunity to bridge generational divides and create lasting family memories. Such trips are not mere vacations; they are immersive experiences that foster understanding and appreciation across ages, providing benefits for both grandparents and younger family members.

For MY grandparents, a family vacation could mean a chance to be the life of the party, sharing stories and laughter. Destinations with a mix of relaxation and adventure, such as a cruise including both days at sea and exciting port excursions, cater to their sociable nature. They can be the historians sharing tales with the young ones or the adventurers trying out new activities.

CD grandparents might appreciate a quieter, scenic getaway, such as a mountain retreat or a trip to a beachfront villa, where the landscape takes center stage. Serene environments allow for deep conversations and shared moments without the hustle of crowded tourist spots. CD grandparents can teach grandchildren to fish or knit, passing on skills in a tranquil setting.

Straddler grandparents might enjoy a vacation that balances activity with downtime, such as a cultural tour through a historic city followed by a leisurely afternoon exploring local cafes. They can engage in a walking tour one day and spend the next painting or photographing their experiences, providing a variety of experiences to suit their ambivert nature.

Regardless of the destination, multi-generational vacations allow grandparents to step into the worlds of their children and grandchildren and experience the wonder through younger eyes. They provide a platform for grandparents to pass on heritage and personal stories, enriching the family's collective narrative.

For the younger generation, these vacations are equally beneficial. They can absorb wisdom and gain a sense of continuity and belonging. Children and adults alike learn patience, empathy, and respect as they accommodate the needs and pace of their elders. Moreover, they receive the gift of time with their grandparents, which is irreplaceable.

The shared experiences gained on a multi-generational vacation are an investment in family bonds. They offer a break from the usual routines and responsibilities of life, allowing all family members to simply enjoy being together. These are the times when family legends are born, when stories that will be told for years are crafted, and when the familial bonds are strengthened.

When planning such a vacation, consider the preferences and physical limitations of the grandparents, ensuring there is ample opportunity for rest and that health considerations are taken into account. The key is to craft an inclusive itinerary that offers something for everyone, balancing rest with adventure and individual exploration with collective experiences.

Plan Family Game Nights

Planning family game nights with grandparents is an excellent way to cultivate a sense of togetherness and foster intergenerational interaction. These gatherings are not just about the games; they are a conduit for laughter, learning, and creating shared memories.

For MY grandparents, game nights are a stage for storytelling and animated competition. Opt for games that are engaging and involve a degree of performance, such as charades, or Pictionary, where they can express their outgoing personalities. These games encourage participation and ensure that MYs can revel in the limelight, sharing their exuberance with the family.

CD grandparents may prefer games that allow for strategic thought and quieter contemplation, such as chess or classic card games. These games provide a comfortable environment for them to demonstrate their skills without the pressure of a boisterous setting. It's a way for CDs to connect deeply with family members, one move at a time.

Straddler grandparents can enjoy a balance between high-energy games and those requiring more thought. Trivia games that span various eras can be ideal, as they allow Straddlers to showcase their knowledge and engage in light-hearted competition. Games that involve teams also work well, allowing them to oscillate between leading and supporting roles.

In planning these game nights, consider games that are inclusive and adaptable to various skill levels and physical abilities. Ensure that everyone can participate meaningfully, whether by rolling dice, reading out questions, or keeping score. It's important to choose games that encourage collaboration and communication, allowing family members to work together and learn from one another.

Family game nights can also serve as an educational exchange, with grandparents sharing games from their youth and grandchildren introducing modern or digital games. This exchange of past and present gaming experiences can be a valuable learning opportunity for both generations.

For the younger generation, these nights are a chance to learn valuable life skills such as fair play, strategic thinking, and patience. They learn to celebrate wins gracefully and handle losses with composure, guided by the wisdom and demeanor of their grandparents.

Ultimately, the objective of family game nights is to ensure that everyone leaves the table with a smile. It's about the warmth of shared victories, the hilarity of playful disputes, and the silent pact that these nights will be a cherished tradition, eagerly anticipated by all ages. It's about weaving a tapestry of familial love, one game at a time, in an atmosphere filled with joy and camaraderie.

Revisit Places of Significance

Taking grandparents to revisit places that hold special meaning in their lives is a profound way to honor their past and deepen familial bonds.

These journeys to significant places—be it an old neighborhood, a cherished park, or a cultural landmark—can be a deeply moving experience for both the older and younger generations.

For MY grandparents, such excursions are an opportunity to share stories of their more exuberant days and allows them to recount lively tales of past adventures or community gatherings. They might relish the chance to show where they once lived life to the fullest, sharing anecdotes that animate their history with color and vivacity.

CD grandparents might approach these visits more introspectively, reflecting on how these places have shaped their quiet reflections and personal growth over the years. They may share memories of tranquil solitude or moments of deep personal significance, offering a glimpse into the more private aspects of their lives.

Straddler grandparents, balancing between introspection and extroversion, might provide a rich narrative that weaves both the quiet, meaningful moments with the more public, shared experiences. They can offer a unique perspective that captures the essence of these places in all their facets.

When planning these visits, it's important to engage in conversations that encourage grandparents to express what these places mean to them, prompting them to share memories and insights. It's equally important to facilitate the visit in a way that is comfortable for them, taking into account mobility considerations and allowing for rest as needed.

For the younger family members, these visits are an invaluable lesson in their heritage and personal history. They learn about their grandparents' lives within the context of different times, gaining insights into how the world has changed and what has remained important through the years.

Moreover, revisiting these significant places is not just about reflecting on the past; it's about creating new memories in these old haunts. It's an opportunity to bring the past into the present, connecting generations through shared experience and mutual reverence for the family's collective history.

Ultimately, these shared pilgrimages to places of significance reinforce the continuum of family legacy. They serve as a reminder that while time moves forward, the places that have shaped us remain a testament to our journey. For grandparents, it's a chance to relive cherished moments, and for the younger generation, it's an opening to build upon the family narrative with newfound respect and understanding.

Key Takeaways

This chapter underscores the value of maintaining and nurturing connections with grandparents, recognizing the diverse ways in which MY, CD, and Straddler grandparents engage with their adult grandchildren.

- **Appreciate Generational Wisdom:** Acknowledge the wealth of knowledge and experience that grandparents, regardless of their temperament, bring to the family dynamic. Valuing their insights encourages a rich exchange of wisdom across generations.

- **Cultivate Emotional Connections:** Whether your grandparents are outgoing MYs, contemplative CDs, or lie somewhere in between, fostering emotional bonds is key. Tailor your approach to suit their personalities, ensuring they feel connected and cherished.

- **Prioritize Inclusivity:** In planning activities, be it family vacations or game nights, consider the preferences and capabilities of all generations. This inclusivity promotes a sense of belonging and enjoyment for grandparents and grandchildren alike.

- **Encourage Shared Experiences:** Create opportunities for grandparents to impart their legacy and for grandchildren to share their own stories. This two-way exchange deepens understanding and respect between generations.

- **Adapt Communication:** Strive for clear, considerate communication that respects both the wisdom of age and the perspectives of youth. Open dialogue bridges the gap between generations and fosters harmonious relationships.

- **Embrace Tradition and Innovation:** Balance revisiting places of significance with exploring new activities together. This harmony of past and present enriches the family narrative and builds a foundation for future memories.

- **Recognize the Role of Physical Affection:** Understand the importance of physical gestures, such as hugs, in conveying love and respect, while also respecting individual comfort levels with physical affection.

By embracing these key takeaways, you'll be equipped to build and sustain a meaningful relationship with your grandparents. It's a reciprocal journey where understanding and love are shared, where the past is honored and new memories are forged, ensuring that every family member's unique contribution is celebrated in the ongoing story of your family.

Chapter Eight

Final Thoughts

In the boundless landscape of human connections, love rises as one of our most profound yet complex experiences. It is far more than fleeting moments of shared joy or the warmth of a comforting embrace; love is a commitment to growth, understanding, and standing stoically together. In these pages, we have embarked on an enlightening expedition through the intricate world of loving a Cave Dweller, Mountain Yeller, or Straddler grandparent. Now, let us pause to appreciate all we have learned on this odyssey of the heart.

Understanding the Depth of Personality

Every individual is a unique cosmos of thoughts, emotions, and perspectives. Your CD grandparent may find sanctuary in silent spaces, their introspective nature thriving inwardly, while your MY grandparent revels in lively social spheres, expressing themselves outwardly with zeal. Though seemingly opposite, these differences can paint a beautiful mosaic when appreciated. Remember our discussions on active listening, appreciating quietude, and offering verbal affirmations? These are not merely guidance strategies. They are passageways to comprehension, empathy, and profound connection.

Peeling back the layers to see someone's authentic essence is the pinnacle of understanding.

The Unwavering Commitment of Love

Love is not fleeting, it is steadfast. It is not a single grand gesture, but a daily renewal of choice. Recall the tools we discovered together—reconfirming bonds, planning surprise outings, seeking family counseling, and prioritizing quality time. These are not just actions, but representations of an unwavering commitment to nurture the living, breathing bond you share. Like a flowering plant, love requires daily care and watering to continue blossoming.

The Adaptive Nature of Lasting Love

Change is inevitable, and in familial relationships, it can signify growth, wisdom, and mutual understanding. Consider the dance between CD and MY personalities—their harmony requires flexibility, balance, and adjustment. Our discussions around financial planning, and establishing traditions and rituals were about more than checking tasks off a list. They embodied embracing change, adapting together, and finding joy in evolution.

Celebrating Diversity Through Unity

There is remarkable splendor in two distinct souls coming together under one roof. The combination of a CD's introspection with an MY's exuberance breeds something uniquely beautiful. Remember our conversations on customizing celebrations, trying new hobbies, and revisiting meaningful places? These are not just moments, but milestones where differences unite to create harmonious new memories.

The Journey of Personal and Mutual Growth

Growth is the essence of life. In family, it is the adhesive that binds members through time. Reflect on the times you have buoyed your grandparents' ambitions, championed their dreams, or embarked on a quest of mutual understanding. Growth is about acknowledging that as individuals, and as a family unit, there is always room for progress, adaptation, and cultivation to become better versions of ourselves.

The Boundless Horizons of Love

The insights covered in these pages are but a glimpse into love's vast and marvelous landscape. Your unique voyage with a CD, MY, or Straddler grandparent brims with its own challenges, joys, and unforgettable moments. While this guide has armed you with knowledge, every new day offers fresh lessons, experiences, and memories to integrate into your daily life. Use these words as your compass but let your heart chart the course.

The Continuing Evolution of Your Love Story

As we conclude, remember that your bond with your grandparent is an ever-evolving tale, marked with unique challenges, triumphs, highs, and lows. The shared moments, lessons learned, and obstacles overcome make this journey distinctly yours. Absorb the insights acquired, treasure every interaction, and look forward with enthusiasm to the myriad experiences yet to unfold. The connection with your grandparents, in all its depth and nuance, is an expedition worth pursuing with all your heart. Progress with understanding, patience, and unyielding commitment.

Appendices

Self-Assessment Questionnaire: Determine Whether You're a CD, MY, or Straddler.

In the quest for self-understanding, recognizing one's intrinsic personality traits plays a crucial role. This self-assessment questionnaire has been carefully designed to help you discern whether you align most closely with the introspective nature of a Cave Dweller (CD), the extroverted inclinations of a Mountain Yeller (MY), or the balanced characteristics of a Straddler. By reflecting on your behaviors, preferences, and reactions in various situations, this tool aims to provide insight into your predominant personality type. Approach each question with honesty and openness, and remember, there's no right or wrong answer—just a deeper understanding of your unique self waiting to be unveiled.

Personality Indicator #1

Circle one answer per question.

1. Have you ever walked in your sleep during your adult life?

   YES or NO

2. As a teenager, did you feel comfortable expressing your feelings to one or both of your parents?

   YES or NO

3. Do you have a tendency to look directly into a person's eyes when talking to them?

   YES or NO

4. Do you feel that most people, when you first meet them, are uncritical of your appearance?

   YES or NO

5. In a group situation with people you've just met, would you feel comfortable drawing attention to yourself by initiating a conversation?

   YES or NO

6. Do you feel comfortable holding hands or hugging someone you're in a relationship with in front of other people?

   YES or NO

7. When someone talks about feeling warm physically, do you begin to feel warm also?

   YES or NO

8. Do you tend to tune out when someone is talking to you because you're anxious to come up with your side of the story?

YES or NO

9. Do you feel that you learn better by seeing and/or reading than by hearing?

YES or NO

10. In a new class or company meeting, do you usually feel comfortable asking questions in front of the group?

YES or NO

11. When expressing your ideas, do you find it important to relate all the details leading up to the subject so the other person can understand it completely?

YES or NO

12. Do you enjoy relating to children?

YES or NO

13. Are you comfortable with your body movements when faced with unfamiliar people and circumstances?

YES or NO

14. Do you prefer reading fiction rather than non-fiction?

YES or NO

15. If you were to imagine sucking on a juicy lemon, would your mouth water?

    YES or NO

16. Do you feel comfortable receiving a compliment in front of other people?

    YES or NO

17. Do you feel that you're a good conversationalist?

    YES or NO

18. Do you feel comfortable when complimentary attention is drawn to your physical body?

    YES or NO

Personality Indicator # 2

Circle one answer per question.

1. Have you ever awakened in the middle of the night and felt that you could not move your body and/or talk?

    YES or NO

2. As a child, did you feel you were more affected by your parents' tone of voice than by what they actually said?

    YES or NO

3. If someone you know talks about a fear that you've experienced before, do you have a tendency to re-experience that apprehension or fear?

    YES or NO

4. After having an argument with someone, do you tend to dwell on what you could or should have said?

    YES or NO

5. Do you tend to occasionally tune out when someone is talking to you and therefore don't hear what's being said because your mind drifts to something totally unrelated?

    YES or NO

6. Do you sometimes desire to be complimented for a job well done, but feel embarrassed or uncomfortable when

complemented?

YES or NO

7. Do you often fear not being able to carry on a conversation with someone you've just met?

YES or NO

8. Do you feel self-conscious when attention is drawn to your physical body or appearance?

YES or NO

9. If you had a choice, would you rather avoid being around children most of the time?

YES or NO

10. Do you feel uptight in body movements, especially when faced with unfamiliar people or circumstances?

YES or NO

11. Do you prefer reading non-fiction rather than fiction?

YES or NO

12. If someone describes a very bitter taste, do you have difficulty experiencing the physical feeling of that bitter taste?

YES or NO

13. Do you generally feel that you see yourself less favorably than

others see you?

YES or NO

14. Do you tend to feel awkward or self-conscious holding hands and/or kissing someone you're in a relationship with, in front of other people?

YES or NO

15. In a new lecture or company meeting, do you usually feel uncomfortable asking questions in front of the group?

YES or NO

16. Do you feel uneasy if someone you've just met looks you directly in the eyes when talking to you, especially if the conversation is about you?

YES or NO

17. In a group situation with people you've just met, would you feel uncomfortable drawing attention to yourself by initiating a conversation?

YES or NO

18. If you're in a relationship or are very close to someone, do you find it difficult or embarrassing to verbalize your love for them?

YES or NO

Personality Indicator Scores

Personality Indicator #1

- Give yourself 10 points for every "yes" answer for questions 1 and 2.

- Give yourself 5 points for every answer for questions 3–18.

- Write the total number at the top of #1's questionnaire.

Personality Indicator #2

- Give yourself 10 points for every "yes" answer for questions 1 and 2.

- Give yourself 5 points for every answer for questions 3–18.

- Write the total number at the top of #2's questionnaire.

- Combine the total from PIs 1 and 2.

Using the Scoring Chart

On the scoring chart, look up the combined score of Personality Indicators 1 and 2 on the HORIZONTAL axis of the chart and circle the number.

- Take the total score of PI #1, locate it on the VERTICAL axis of the chart, and circle the number.

- Draw a horizontal line across the page from the PI 1 score, then draw a vertical line down from the combined score.

- The number in the box where the two lines intersect represents your true, adjusted percentage Personality Indicator.

- Scores 61 and higher indicate a Mountain Yeller personality type.

- Scores 45 and lower indicate a Cave Dweller personality type.

- Scores 47–56 indicate a Straddler personality type.

Cave Dweller Tendencies

- Reserved

- Head ruled

- Controlling

- Wants space and security

- Prefers socializing one-on-one

- Singular focus

- Thinks before reacting

- Prefers showing affection privately

- Distrusts flattery

- Enjoys working alone

- Enjoys individual activities

- Wants alone time

- Dresses for comfort
- Decides after thinking about it
- Speaks literally—to the point
- Infers from what others say
- Feels emotional pain in the mind
- Fears loss of security

Cave Dweller Priorities

- Career/Financial Security
- Hobbies/Children
- Relationships/Family
- Sex/Lovers

Mountain Yeller Tendencies

- Outgoing
- Heart ruled
- Dominating
- Wants connection and touch
- Enjoys socializing in groups
- Moving focus

- Reacts spontaneously
- Comfortable with affection anytime
- Likes reassurance and compliments
- Enjoys working with people
- Enjoys team activities
- Wants to be together as much as possible
- Decides in the moment
- Speaks inferentially—adds story
- Takes literally what others say
- Feels emotional pain in body and mind
- Fears rejection

Mountain Yeller Priorities

- Relationships/Sex
- Family/Children
- Friends/Hobbies
- Career/Financial security

COMBINED SCORE #1 AND #2

SCORE #1 \ #2	50	55	60	65	70	75	80	85	90	95	100	105	110	115	120	125	130	135	140	145	150	155	160	165	170	175	180	185	190	195	200
100											100	95	91	87	83	80	77	74	71	69	67	65	63	61	59	57	56	54	53	51	50
95										100	95	90	86	83	79	76	73	70	68	66	63	61	59	58	56	54	53	51	50	49	48
90									100	95	90	86	82	78	75	72	69	67	64	62	60	58	56	55	53	51	50	48	47	46	45
85								100	94	89	85	81	77	74	71	68	65	63	61	59	57	55	53	52	50	49	47	46	45	44	43
80							100	94	89	84	80	76	73	70	67	64	62	59	57	55	53	52	50	48	47	46	44	43	42	41	40
75						100	94	88	83	79	75	71	68	65	63	60	58	56	54	52	50	48	47	45	44	43	42	41	39	38	38
70					100	93	88	82	78	74	70	67	64	61	58	56	54	52	50	48	47	45	44	42	41	40	39	38	37	36	35
65				100	93	87	81	76	72	68	65	62	59	57	54	52	50	48	46	45	43	42	41	39	38	37	36	35	34	33	33
60			100	92	86	80	75	71	67	63	60	57	55	52	50	48	46	44	43	41	40	39	38	36	35	34	33	32	32	31	30
55		100	92	85	79	73	69	65	61	58	55	52	50	48	46	44	42	41	39	38	37	36	34	33	32	31	31	30	29	28	28
50	100	91	83	77	71	67	63	59	56	53	50	48	45	43	43	40	38	37	36	34	33	32	31	30	29	29	28	27	26	26	25
45	90	82	75	69	64	60	56	53	50	47	45	43	41	39	36	36	35	33	32	31	30	28	27	26	26	25	24	24	23	23	23
40	80	73	67	62	57	53	50	47	44	42	40	38	36	35	33	32	31	30	29	28	27	26	25	24	24	23	22	22	21	21	20
35	70	64	58	54	50	47	44	41	39	37	35	33	32	30	29	28	27	26	25	24	23	23	22	21	21	20	19	19	18	18	18
30	60	55	50	46	43	40	38	35	33	32	30	29	27	26	25	24	23	22	21	21	20	19	19	18	18	17	17	16	16	15	15
25	50	45	42	38	35	33	31	29	28	26	25	24	23	22	21	20	19	19	18	17	17	16	16	15	14	14	14	13	13	13	13
20	40	36	33	31	29	27	25	24	23	21	20	19	18	17	17	16	15	15	14	14	13	13	12	12	11	11	11	11	10	10	10
15	30	27	25	23	21	20	19	18	17	16	15	14	13	13	12	12	11	11	10	10	10	9	9	9	9	8	8	8	8	8	8
10	20	18	17	15	14	13	13	12	11	11	10	10	9	9	8	8	7	7	7	7	6	6	6	6	6	6	5	5	5	5	5
5	10	9	8	8	7	7	6	6	6	5	5	5	4	4	4	4	4	3	3	3	3	3	3	3	3	3	3	3	3	3	3
0	0	0	0	0	0	0	0	0	0	0	0	0	0	0	0	0	0	0	0	0	0	0	0	0	0	0	0	0	0	0	0

About the Author

Dr. Cline lives with her husband, two daughters, two German Shepherds, and two Yorkies in the hills of North Carolina. Her expertise in relationship building has offered her the opportunity to travel around the world as a keynote speaker and international workshop facilitator.

www.ingramcontent.com/pod-product-compliance
Lightning Source LLC
Chambersburg PA
CBHW070107080526
44586CB00013B/1212